A Life Less Lost

Chuck 2009

KB Walker

My son's decision, but will he choose life?

Dedication

To Howard, James and David

Published in 2009 by
Pog Hall Books
539 Manchester Road
Huddersfield HD7 5QX

Printed in the UK

ISBN 978-1-872955-31-5

Disclaimer

This is necessarily my interpretation of events, my story. Others, alongside me on this journey, would probably tell these tales differently. For this reason, I have changed some people's names, including my own. Otherwise, I have tried to share truthfully my experiences.

Acknowledgements

I'm enormously grateful to all those who have listened, encouraged, offered constructive criticism and prayers for me and this project. For all the members of my church, house group, the Huddersfield Authors' Circle, Holmfirth Writers' Group, ACW, Script Yorkshire, Huddersfield Literature Festival Writers, Gang of Five, internet Writers' Forum, Creative Writing classes and Cornerstones Literary Consultancy. An extra thank you is owed to Lindsay, Gale, Joan, Betty, Kate, Sally, Jill and Howard who read various drafts of the manuscript in its entirety.

Special thanks to CIDA and Richard for guiding me through the shark infested waters of self-publishing.

To my wonderful husband, Howard, who made it possible for me to 'have a go', and to my beautiful sons and wider family, who allowed me to share this story with others, I'm humbled by the faith you have in me.

Now glory be to God! By his mighty power at work within us, he is able to accomplish infinitely more than we would ever dare to ask or hope. Ephesians 3.20 NLT

Prologue

Wednesday 29 October 1980

'Gmmn.' The sound of my own groan is enough to shove me through the bits of dream and sleep fog into wakefulness. *Yuck, I'm wet. I've wet the bed!*

I hurry into our tiny bathroom, disgusted and alarmed. The last time I wet a bed was pre-memory. I don't understand what's happening. I've been unwell all weekend, achy and weary, but that can't be it. My first antenatal class will be tonight. The baby isn't due for six and a half more weeks. I'm frightened.

'Howard,' I call from the toilet, 'something's wrong. I've wet the bed and can't stop weeing.'

'You mucky cow,' he says. The bed creaks. 'It's not even six o'clock.' I hear his head flop back down onto the pillow.

'Could you phone the hospital to find out what we should do?' I ask.

'I'm not going to tell someone my wife can't stop weeing!'

I dribble down our narrow stone stairs and phone myself.

'It sounds like your waters have broken,' the nurse tells me. 'An ambulance is on the way.'

My repentant husband is suddenly wide awake and rushing about like any new father in a television sit-com. I dress and run a comb through my wild hair. I'm still leaking.

It takes ages for the ambulance to arrive. We live in an old cottage, in a remote village, on the edge of the hospital's catchment area. The driver suggests Howard lead the way because of his knowledge of the winding country lanes.

Howard speeds off then has to stop and wait for the ambulance, which won't travel much faster than 30 miles an hour for fear of hastening the arrival of the baby. I waddle into the hospital and the soggy seat of my maternity dress slaps against the back of my legs. I feel like a child that's had an accident in class. The doctor examines me and says I'm not in labour and it could be another week but I will have to stay in hospital. He sends Howard off to work.

They're very busy in the maternity ward so I'm put in a bare, little side room on my own. The muscles across my huge bump may not be contracting but I'm struggling with excruciating back pain. I alternate between worrying about the baby and the fact that I don't know how to relax yet. We're supposed to learn that at antenatal class, tonight.

I try to think about how much I've loved being pregnant, couldn't wait to 'show'. Howard and I were both keen that we did everything to help our baby have a good start in life. Neither of us smoked anyway but we cut out alcohol and Howard encouraged me to drink plenty of milk and eat spinach and liver (which I hate).

All the way through my pregnancy I felt I was a month further along than my dates or the doctor indicated. Ultrasound was relatively new and not standard practice. The signposts I read about in the baby books appeared to happen earlier than they should. But you assume doctors know best.

To squash down my rising fear and pain, I try to recall funny things that happened. Like the fact that a couple of my older colleagues at work guessed I was pregnant before I did, when I went off tea and coffee. At least my cravings weren't too bizarre, family sized tins of rice pudding usually satisfied.

Howard looked younger than his twenty four years, probably due to good health and his golden curls. I remember how upset he was, one day, whilst in the local sandwich shop near where he worked. The woman on the till had asked him when the baby was due and the customer behind almost dropped her shopping.

'How old *are* you? she squeaked.

'Well, how old do you think I am?' he replied, quite unprepared for her revelation that she thought he was only fifteen.

I found it hilarious and assured him he would be very grateful when he was forty-five and looked thirty-five.

The howling ache in my back has clawed through every corner of my body now, slashing further memories from its path. I try everything I can think of to cope with the pain, including attempting to remember how to count to a hundred in French. The single window is high and off behind me. There is nothing to read, no one to talk to and nothing to distract me. I'm afraid to move in case it will hurt the baby. I imagine the poor thing trapped inside me without its warm amniotic bath to cushion against bumps and bangs.

By afternoon, the torture becomes unbearable. I can't stand it any longer and ring the bell for help.

A very harassed midwife huffs in and snaps on some rubber gloves. 'We're very busy, you know.' She pulls my legs up and examines me.

'The head, the head!'

Suddenly, everything is in motion and I'm hurtling down the corridor on my bed. The delivery suite isn't ready so I'm parked in a tiny, windowless side room with a young nurse. I can't think beyond the agony and plead for relief. The nurse gives me an injection of Pethadin, which she shouldn't have, apparently, so close to delivery. It sends me spinning into space.

Meanwhile, Howard has sorted things out at work for this unexpected event and returns as soon as he is able to be by my side. We'd talked about whether he should be present at the birth but being exceptionally squeamish about blood, he wasn't sure he could do it. He's been known to pass out just having his blood pressure taken. But when the nurses see him walk in through the hospital doors, they press a shower cap thing on his head, plastic bags on his feet and push him into the room.

I'm so relieved to see him that I want to cry. The drugs have made me loud and gushy. The delivery room is full of people because they expect the baby to be premature but I feel almost invisible. There are specialist nurses, a midwife, paediatrician and heaven only knows who else, all busy doing their jobs around me. Thank goodness the Pethadin and the pain have removed my inhibitions or I don't think I could bear lying there with my legs in the air, naked from the waist down.

A masked person leans over and asks, 'Do you mind if these twelve student midwives come in to watch?'

'Sure, why not?' It all seems unreal and I don't care what they do anymore, as long as they get this baby out as soon as possible. But poor Howard is embarrassed on my behalf. He unsuccessfully tries to shush my shrieks.

After the head, the shoulders slip through with a last push. The baby is whisked away and panic creeps into my spinning mind. I can't even feel the stitches they're putting in where I was cut to ease the passage.

When James is finally in my arms, breathing on his own, with all his fingers and toes, I'm euphoric, far beyond the effect of the painkiller. He's so tiny, so perfect that I'm overwhelmed by the responsibility of his care. My body feels full to bursting with electric sunshine and gratitude to God for this precious child.

The baby isn't, as it turns out, six weeks premature. I'd been right about being a month further along. As good, hardworking and clever as doctors are, it's worth knowing they don't always get it right.

Chapter 1

Despite rain today, the school purrs with summer lethargy. The air is warm and damp, heavy with the smell of children. The term is winding down, only finishing off, tidying up and final assemblies stand between us and the six-week break. Howard hasn't booked our holiday, yet. This is almost unheard of but things have been crazy for him at work and we've had to cancel one trip already this year.

Because of the weather, my playground duty is indoors. I reflect on my recent interview for a deputy headship, as I patrol the classrooms. The feedback had been positive and I'd just missed out, apparently. But the whole process, of deciding to change jobs, 'selling myself' in the application and preparing for the presentation and interview, has given me a boost. I feel more confident and optimistic about my future.

I move from room to room, reassuring the timid and the attention seekers. A little girl, 5 or 6 years old, accompanies me. She's tiny for her age and speaks limited English. Two larger girls have been picking on her.

Another child comes to tell me that I'm wanted on the phone, in the office – this is unusual. Apprehension buzzes beneath my skin. I hold my companion's small hand a little tighter and hurry along the shiny corridor. All appears normal in the cupboard-sized room. The secretary moves about her business amongst tidy clutter.

'The consultant wants to see us in two hours, without James.'

Howard's voice tries to hold me, to shield me but it's too late. Panic squeezes my lungs, recalls the blood from my limbs and screams in my ears. My eyelids are ripped open and I'm forced to see all the warning signs I'd buried. I know instantly what I cannot bear to believe. My son has cancer.

*

Watch news coverage of any disaster and you will see people searching for something or someone to blame, desperate to believe it's possible to prevent catastrophes. Now, with the binoculars of hindsight I can see the tiptoed footprints of Terror; hear the echoes of its whispers. But then, my eyes and ears were firmly closed. Everything in me resisted even a tiny peek at the possibilities it was suggesting.

In the autumn of 1995, James would come to us, usually at night, to say his leg hurt. These pains seemed to come and go and vary in intensity. He didn't want us to touch it when it was sore but the next day, when it didn't hurt, he wouldn't let us fuss him. He was a busy, active fifteen-year-old so we thought it must be a forgotten sporting injury or bump, then possibly 'growing pains' or the result of being run down.

As part of my fortieth birthday celebrations, Howard, James, David and I went to America for the holidays. It was only the second time I'd been 'home' for Christmas in eighteen years.

We had a wonderful but different kind of celebration with my dad, two brothers, stepsister and their families, in Michigan. My brother, Keith, kept in touch with my first stepmother, Nicki, and his wife's parents were divorced with new partners so their extended family arrangements were very complicated, as several of these adults couldn't bear to see one another.

After a few days of playing in the snow and catching up with my family we flew on to Arizona to spend some time in the sunshine with my dad and his wife, Lynda, in their winter home. I didn't suspect a thing when they took us out for a meal on my birthday and my friend Christine and her family were there, all the way from England. They travelled with us the next day to the Grand Canyon. Despite having seen photos and even a 360-degree film of it, my knees buckled at the sight.

But the pains in James' leg persisted after our holiday away and appeared to be getting worse. I wanted to take him to the doctor but we couldn't seem to find a time that would be convenient, when neither of us had a commitment.

Finally, I received a phone call at work to say that someone had poked James in the eye, which had swollen shut. The school nurse felt he should see a doctor immediately. I downed tools, collected him and took him to our GP. Thankfully, his eye was fine but while we were there, we asked about his leg. The doctor checked him over and to my horror declared there was definitely something abnormal and he would refer James for an x-ray.

The x-ray technician bounced into the room and said, "Don't worry, lad, this will only take a minute". Returning, he was a changed man and told James he needed a few more pictures. We experienced brief fluttery panic when we went back to the doctor and he reported that he didn't think it was cancer but it was worrying. Cancer was an obscenity we hadn't allowed to cross our minds and since it had been dismissed, we quickly shut it out again.

James was then referred to a consultant and given CT and MRI scans. We were told it was an osteoblastoma or benign growth, like a wart on his bone, which should go away on its own. If the pains became worse, he could return and it would be surgically removed.

Relieved that everything seemed to be OK, we all got on with our lives, each of us busy at work or school, meeting friends, enjoying social events. On a brief holiday in the Lake District, James seemed to struggle with the walking we normally all enjoyed. We alternated between being sympathetic and exasperated with the pain he occasionally complained about.

To understand our exasperation you need to know a bit more about James. As he approached high school age, we seemed to visit casualty more and more frequently. The first time, he'd been playing on a rope swing and crashed into the tree. I looked at his arm but it wasn't swollen and he had full movement in his fingers. It wasn't until the next day that I took him to the hospital. What kind of mother tells her son off for playing in his best trousers and makes him do his piano practice with a broken arm?

The following year, a punch to my younger son David's head resulted in a broken hand for James and a trip to see an orthopaedic surgeon to patch him up. A few months later, he broke his arm on a scout trip. Once again the arm didn't swell and no one believed him. He was teased and told to stop whining. One boy even yanked on it and asked if it hurt. The next day the scout leader walked him to the local GP who sent him on by ambulance to the hospital where he had to be anaesthetised so that they could pull and twist it back into place.

A week after having his pot off James was back in casualty. Tripping over a curb, he smashed into a wall and lacerated his face, bruised his knee, shoulder and wrist. When he fell off a wall, we were all interviewed to eliminate the possibility that James was the victim of child abuse. In the meantime, he'd been hard at work devising other ingenious ways to hurt himself. For instance, whilst ironing naked (like you do) he turned quickly and burnt his stomach. Or there was the time he managed to get a video box stuck on his eyelashes…

James' asthma wasn't improving with age either. He didn't/couldn't/ wouldn't remember to take his inhaler regularly. He was susceptible to hay fever and minor colds would get into his lungs and set up germ cities. None of it had any impact on his approach to life. He played badminton, football, basketball, roller hockey, swam, played the piano, was active in scouts, took part in school plays and excelled at school.

David, was equally active but, thankfully, with a lot less drama. Quieter, he'd long since learned that getting a word in edgewise in his noisy family was impossible. He displayed a healthy respect for his body, ran in the cross-country team, swam, played badminton, was just as busy with the scouts and in high school took up the saxophone and joined the music centre. By eleven, he'd been captivated by jazz and was beginning to expand and develop his wide taste in music.

After our walking holiday, the pains began to get much worse and James decided he wanted the operation the consultant had mentioned earlier in the year. He reacted very badly to the anaesthetic and was dreadfully sick. The doctor was in a big rush to get away and tried to leave the room three times before I'd finished asking my questions. Fortunately, I'd been advised to write them down in advance. Excellent advice, as you can't always think clearly under pressure.

A few weeks later, for David's fourteenth birthday, we celebrated over a weekend. On Saturday, he took several friends to laser quest and bowling then home for cake and ice cream. Sunday was a quiet family party with lunch out at a nearby hotel. There had certainly been no warning, in the laughter and chatter or the game of snooker on a sun-warmed table, of what the next day would bring.

***

I slump into the office chair and try to speak. My throat is choked and only cracked partial words escape. The little girl's eyes round with fear and she backs into the secretary's silent grasp. I put the phone down. I can't explain. 'We have to meet the consultant without our son' doesn't seem to justify my reaction. But I can't say that other word out loud.

I'm at work. The fragments of my old life remind me there are things to do. Like wreckage in a storm, I want to grip on to them. Somehow, I'm back in my classroom trying to read a story to thirty 6 and 7 year olds. Immediately, they sense a change.

'Have you been crying?'

'Why?'

'James will be OK, though, won't he?'

Their questions go right to the heart of the matter. I manage to get through the half hour to home time. The children don't know any platitudes so offer instead small, sad smiles. Many touch my hand or hug my waist on their way out.

My boss materialises. Gently, she says, 'take whatever time you need.'

I know I should be grateful but I panic. I want to escape in the familiar. The demands of teaching young children are so intense you can feel like you operate in two parallel existences, one at work and the other outside work. I mumble.

She is wise enough to leave her offer open until I'm ready. She can also see that I'm too fragile for anything else. Silently, she leaves.

Frantically, mechanically I busy myself. Then it's time.

Howard and I sit beside each other, separately locked in our own fears.

The man, who only a few months ago told us it was nothing to worry about, looks distressed and uncomfortable. He won't meet my eyes or give definite answers. I am paralysed with pain.

An appointment has been made for us, later in the week, with Dr Edwards[1], a leading paediatric oncologist based in a teaching hospital in Leeds. We drive home alone, each in our own car having come straight from work. We ·tell the boys. Push food around plates. James insists we keep it secret until he's met the oncologist, not ready to believe what the appointment implies until the details are spelled out.

Howard and I go to Parent's Night. We listen in agony, as the teachers tell us what a wonderful, clever boy James is and that he needs to make sure he works hard next year for the all-important GCSE exams.

In bed, my eyes won't close. My skin and muscles prickle with the fight or flight instinct. But who can I fight, where can I run? Under attack, we've curled in on ourselves. Unable to comfort one another, we lie side by side in shocked silence.

I tiptoe into James' room. He's awake, full of hard questions with no answers. I bring him back to our room to lie between us. But he's as tall as I am and I have to cling to the edge until I hear his breathing deepen. I finally sleep in his bed, taking an irrational comfort in knowing he is safe with his dad.

*

On New Year's Eve 1976, my twenty-first birthday, I was home alone making a winter coat for my trip to England. My friends were scattered around Michigan and other family members were out with their friends. My belongings had been brought back to my dad's house, from university, for the last time. All I would need, for my four-month teaching practice in Yorkshire, was packed for the journey.

I never really liked New Year's Eve. The foot-stamping, self-centred child in me blamed 'her' for stealing the special-ness of my birthday. A

1, Not his real name

disturbance, as I fell off to sleep, reminded me of another reason I wasn't keen. My fourteen-year-old step-sister had arrived home and was vomiting in the bathroom. I managed to manhandle her into the bath, shower the filth off then dump her into bed. Black thoughts grumbled out of me, as I cleaned up the mess.

The flight from Detroit to London was long and I was wearied as much by my nerves as by the journey. Sometimes it seemed as though there were two of me, one that signed up for adventures and the other who had to go on them, amazed to find herself there.

I located the bus into London from the metropolis that is Heathrow and, struggling with heavy bags, made my way to the accommodation information desk at Kings Cross station. I wasn't due to meet the other exchange students until the next day and hadn't booked anywhere to stay overnight.

'I'm sorry, there are no more single rooms available.' The woman behind the desk announced to the person in front of me in the queue. She didn't appear to be sorry at all, more bored and fed up with the never ending supply of poorly-prepared tourists she had to deal with.

Panic rushed through me. I had visions of freezing to death on a park bench, being robbed and raped.

'Would you consider sharing a room with me?' A heavily accented voice penetrated my fear.

'There aren't any rooms,' I babbled, when I realised the Middle Eastern woman behind was speaking to me. She was old enough to be my mother and had warm, kind eyes.

'There aren't any *single* rooms,' she said, gently.

She spoke to the woman on the desk and booked a double room for the two of us. It was perfect for me, as I felt safer and it was cheaper. We shared easy conversation, which filled our evening.

More luggage-lugging, the next day, and a coach journey north among yet more strangers brought me finally to my destination.

Wentworth Castle College of Education, Barnsley, was a world away from home, literally and figuratively. It didn't look like the Disneyland, fairy-tale kind of castle but it was impressive all the same. Rebuilt and renamed in 1708, it was older than the United States. It sat grandly at the top of a hill surrounded by forty acres of historic gardens. We walked in through enormous double doors into a vast hall with wide, twin staircases curving upwards like embracing arms. Between them stood a carved brass gong the size of a table.

I was allotted a large sunny room on the third floor, once probably servants' quarters. My roommates were a quiet girl from London and a lively girl from Newcastle, whose accent I could barely understand.

I was restless and felt like an intruder so, after introductions, I set off to explore nearby Barnsley. There wasn't a lot to see and soon I was trying to negotiate my way round the unfamiliar bus station to find a way back to the college. '*What am I doing here?*' kept repeating like a mantra in my mind. I was lost amongst busy people rushing confidently around me.

My shabby hooded sweatshirt and short, dark hair, that I cut myself, were probably only two of many signs that announced that I was a foreigner.

'Are you one of the exchange students from the college?'

The Yorkshire voice drew my eyes from the incomprehensible signs above the bus bays. Two fair-haired young men were grinning at me.

'We're on our way up to the college now, if you want to join us.'

I was pleased to have their company and chatter and especially relieved to know I was on the right bus. As we parted company, they invited me to join them and some of the other students in the pub later.

The Stamford Arms was unlike the strident, frantic nightclubs in the university town I'd come from, with their 'conquest' games and superficial contact. The pub was a maze of small cosy rooms with roaring coal fires, shining brasses and baffling unwritten rules of etiquette. There was a snug and a 'men only' room, darts and dominoes to play and 'rounds' of drinks to buy.

Despite not knowing my fellow American students or any of the English ones, I quickly felt comfortable. There was plenty of light-hearted banter, as the lads tried to find a drink I would like. I could recall tasting one, when I was in England two years earlier, that was warm and smooth as honey but I couldn't remember what it was called. Eventually, they decided it must be mead but it wasn't sold in this pub.

There were 25,000 students at my university in Michigan, 500 or so at this college. Already, I felt less anonymous then I did during the three and a half years I lived in Kalamazoo. Perhaps in a smaller group, people on their own are noticed and attempts made to draw them in.

With a thrill of excitement, I realised one of the two men from the bus station, Howard, the one with the blue eyes and curly blonde hair, was interested in me. Considering my pale, freckled face, unruly hair, scruffy clothes and generally scrawny appearance, this was nothing short of amazing.

'I'll walk you back up to college,' he offered, when I tried unsuccessfully to stifle another yawn. The male students were housed in another building in town so it was out of his way but the path back to the college was lonely and went through a stretch of woodland.

'Thank you, I would really appreciate that.'

It was magical walking through the moon-dazzled snow that had fallen whilst we were in the pub. We chatted and laughed and threw snowballs, exhilarated by the crisp night air and the chemistry between us. Little alarm bells began to ring in my mind. There were only twelve guys and 500 or so girls studying at this college and he was fun, charming and gorgeous. My plans were to be in England for four months then back home to work and study for my master's degree in Florida.

'Are you the local lady-killer?' I asked, as he held me in his arms. But I could no sooner resist that first kiss or control my feelings than make the snow stop falling.

We arranged to meet in the morning. I was to give him a lesson in swimming crawl-stroke in exchange for being shown the local sights. I was very self-conscious about my body and used to swim in my jeans and tee-shirt when I was a teen. I changed as quickly as I could in an effort to be in the pool before Howard but he still beat me to it. Luckily for me, without his long-distance glasses, I looked sufficiently fuzzy that he wasn't put off.

It didn't take me long to become accustomed to taking baths instead of showers and responding to the massive gong that summoned us to the four enormous meals we were given each day in the sumptuous dining rooms. ·After surviving on homemade granola cereal, yoghurt and fruit for the previous four months, it was a miracle I wasn't the shape of the gong by the end of the first week.

I discovered a new way of life. Howard introduced me to walking as a pastime and not just a means to an end. We spent many glorious hours hiking through woodland, round sparkling reservoirs and over rolling moorland. I always found it easier to talk to someone without looking at him or her and this was the perfect opportunity to get to know one another. There were no distractions and it was just the two of us surrounded by peace and beauty. I was enthralled by his knowledge of the plants and animals we saw but really showed myself up when Howard made a comment about 'dickey birds' and I asked him how he knew it was a dickey bird.

From the beginning, Howard and I spent every bit of time available to us, together. It was as if we were two parts of a whole and I had found my home, yet was seeing everything through brand new eyes. All the clichés were true. Within two weeks, we were talking about marriage, as naturally as if reading each other's minds.

Of course, it wasn't quite so clear-cut for everyone else. Friends, family, college tutors, even the dinner ladies couldn't fail to register what was happening between us. I'd never had so many letters from my dad before, as he began to realise I might not come back. The college were anxious about any perceived responsibility and we were summoned to 'serious chats' with a number of important people. The dinner ladies were aghast that one of their favourites would choose an American girl when there were so many 'English roses' available.

Neither were we insensitive to the difficulties before us. At a time when divorce rates continued to climb, we knew marriage was a huge step for anyone to take. I couldn't imagine my life without Howard, but would I be able to settle in a strange country, away from all of my family, and forever be a little bit different from everyone else? I was once at a function with Howard when a 'friend' of his told me, quite calmly, that he hated all Americans (a miniscule peek at prejudice).

We joked about the fact that Howard was exactly nine months younger than me, saying that God must have whispered to his mum and dad to get a move on, as I was already here. But there was a part of me that knew this was God's will for me and I wondered at His plan for my life.

***

Robot-like, somehow we get through the week and manage to keep James' secret. On Friday, he and his dad meet with Dr Edwards. As part of the oncologist's excellent practice, his nurse writes down everything that is discussed in the meeting. This is incredibly helpful because there is only so much your brain can take in when it's being pummelled by terrifying facts and information. He offers answers to questions we haven't even thought of yet.

Back home and armed with these notes, Howard calls David and me to join them in the lounge to hear what the doctor had to say.

David refuses to come. Slamming his door, he tries to hide in the security of his bedroom. We begin to realise how much he is suffering. Quieter than his brother, he's never been comfortable talking about his feelings. Eventually, we persuade him to join us but he is silent, his tall, thin frame crumpled in a chair, his face stiff and stony.

Howard tells us that the doctor was open, brutally honest and encouraged them to believe we will all be part of the team that will work to help James get well. They think the cancer is Ewing's Sarcoma or pPNET and that James has a better than average chance of survival but he will need follow up checks for the rest of his life. 'Cures' are not spoken of in relation to cancer, Dr Edwards has told them, firmly.

These words lift and stab. 'Getting James well' and 'better-than-average chance' are phrases that sing out to me but I want a solid clean bill of health, a guarantee. 'Cure' is the cement I think we need to fix our shattered world, to return to that confident sense of safety from this overwhelming danger.

James doesn't have anything to add. He sits quietly, stunned by the day. Howard continues to explain that a full range of tests, to determine an exact diagnosis and to discover if there are other cancers anywhere else, will be done first. These are booked to begin on Tuesday.

A new wave of panic sucks the air from my lungs. I'd never even considered that this evil predator might be eating my son alive from more than one place in his body.

Together, we agree that we will need all the support we can get so we plan to keep our family and friends fully informed. David vanishes back to his room and we suspect he isn't ready to talk to his friends. We don't push him.

Dialling my dad's number, I remember the excited phone call I made years earlier to let him know that he would be a grandfather. He'd guessed my surprise before I could get the words out. Now, I wish with all my heart that I didn't have to tell him about this threat to his beloved grandson. It won't be any easier to tell Howard's mother, a task we will have to do face to face. We are a large, close family; between us we have eight brothers and sisters (not including their partners), seventeen nieces and nephews, ten aunts and uncles and many cousins.

James speaks to each of his friends separately before the news becomes general knowledge. He is open and honest and encourages them to ask questions. He is able to convey how much he needs them to be as normal as possible, to be his friends. I can only praise God for blessing James with the friendships of these lads. You hear a lot about teenage troublemakers but these fifteen-year-old boys are absolutely fantastic.

Howard and I tell our badminton friends in the changing rooms after the game. Despite their obvious shock and dismay, we can feel their concern and desperation to help us. Tony takes Howard to one side in a quiet moment and offers him the precious 'lucky coin' that he's kept for nearly 35 years, since going into the merchant navy at fifteen.

*

Howard and I were anxious to get on the housing ladder, once we were married and both working. We felt rent was money lost and our flat, with its flooded, rat-infested basement and pink, bottom-nipping plastic bathroom suite, was hardly a dream location. Given our financial situation, we started quite near the bottom rung. We dreamed of finding a derelict farmhouse somewhere out on the moors and becoming self-sufficient.

Happily, with hindsight, we found a tiny, stone cottage built in 1824, in a lovely village between Barnsley and Holmfirth. Technically, it was a semi-detached house but in reality it was shorter and smaller than the other part of the building and only about 10cm from the row of terraced houses next door. It had a coal fire, stank of cats and to reach the small back garden you had to go out the front door, walk down the road, up the farmer's lane and across a field.

We bought it for £6,500 and in the three years we lived there we dug out all the plaster three feet up on the ground floor, put in a damp-proof course, re-plastered, added a gas fire, back door, new kitchen, shower, shed, raised flower bed, fencing and re-decorated throughout. We did all but the specialised work ourselves, with a little help from Howard's family, saving up for each new job in between. Those were the days before easy credit and instant access were common. We'd been brought up to believe that debt (excluding mortgages) was akin to leprosy, something to be avoided. I can still remember the thrill of pleasure each time I saw the new net curtains I'd saved up for.

We sold that house for double what we'd paid and moved to a larger end terrace, when James was just over a year old and I was pregnant with David. Many of my peers had grown up in the village; their childhood friends, mothers, aunties, grandparents and sisters lived locally. They weren't all that interested in making new friends. Perhaps it was also that I hadn't quite assimilated enough, but I was lonely. The more I tried to convince these women that I was worth the effort of friendship the more I'm sure I put them off. Sometimes I would cringe when I recalled comments I'd made about myself, recognising the truth in what my mom had told me of the insecurity of show-offs.

After David was born, I joined a Mums and Toddlers group held in the church hall. The boys loved it and I met a very special person called Christine. Petite and fair, she was also a 'comer-in' and had a son that was a year older than James and a baby daughter a month younger than David. We hadn't been friends long when she said she'd been reading in a magazine that spouses that do things together have a better chance of staying together. After much discussion, we settled on badminton. As neither of us knew how to play, we signed up for a course at the local sports centre. It was great fun and I'm sure my stomach muscles got more exercise from the laughter than the actual badminton.

At about this same time, my incredible in-laws came to visit us. Geoffrey, Howard's dad, was small and wiry. A Thespian at heart, he was energy on legs. Howard's mum, Cynthia, was softer, more practical and packed with common sense.

'We think it's important for married couples to have time to themselves,' Mum explained. 'It's all too easy to focus your lives on your children and your jobs but one of the best things you can do for your children is to keep your marriage healthy. We'd like to offer you a regular, weekly night out. Would Friday nights be any good?'

These wonderful people would join us for tea then stay on to baby-sit whilst Howard and I met our friends for badminton. Christine's husband, Tony, and Howard already knew how to play and they tried hard to be patient with us as we learned. The drinks and chat at the pub afterwards were as important as the exercise we got on the court. Over the years we added other couples to our group, Pat and Dave, Ed and Lyn, Tim and Hazel. We all had children of similar ages and shared our worries and delights, enjoyed parties and holidays together.

***

I can't sleep, can barely breath and am struggling to eat. My brain is full of screamed obscenities. I make an appointment to see my GP.

'We don't really want to start down that path, yet,' he tells me gently, when I ask if he can give me something to help with the anxiety. 'I think we should wait and see if things get worse.'

I'm unable to contemplate *things getting worse* and frantically try to bury thoughts of what that implies. It's clear he's desperate to help but he's a good doctor and doesn't prescribe lightly.

'I'll write you a sick note for the final nine days of term,' he offers.

It isn't what I want. Miraculous, medical magic is what I crave, a pill to make everything better. I'm afraid to let go of my 'normal' routine but feel unexpectedly lighter to have one whole chunk of my life lifted from my shoulders. Now I am free to concentrate on helping James and David, if he'll let me.

On Tuesday, James and I set off to the hospital for what we'd been told will be a range of tests and operations to put a portacath in, biopsy a lymph node in his groin and take bone marrow samples from his spine. A portacath is a little metal cup they insert just under the skin below the armpit. It has a tube running up to the neck, where it enters a vein, straight into the heart. It means that the chemo, blood tests and other drugs can be administered directly into this instead of sticking endless needles anywhere else.

Tears wet my face and blur my vision most of the way to the hospital.

'Why are you crying, Mum? I'm going to get well.' It's a cross between a statement of challenge and a question.

I've always tried to be honest and open with my children but I can't bear to bruise his hope or cause his resolve to falter. 'I know you'll get well, sweetheart.' *Please God, let it be so,* I plead in my head.

'I cry at cartoons like Dumbo so there's no chance I can hold my tears back now.' I try a smile but it feels stiff and artificial.

When we arrive on the ward, none of the promised tests have been booked. There is no bed for James and we are left in a playroom for an hour and a half whilst they try to sort something out for us. James, expecting an operation, has had nothing to eat and his leg is incredibly painful. There seems to be no urgency in any of this, whilst all I can think about is the cancer multiplying exponentially and spreading throughout his body.

Eventually, we're sent to another hospital, in a different part of Leeds, for tests on his heart as a baseline to monitor any possible side effects of the chemotherapy. Driving to Leeds has been bad enough, searching for this unknown hospital in an unfamiliar, busy city just adds to the apprehension I already feel.

*

In the summer that I was 15, I took the drivers' education class held at the high school during the long holiday. It was quite a comprehensive course. We were taught how to change tyres, did simulations of night driving and had lectures and quizzes on theory, as well as practical hands-on experience, including motorway driving. My dad supplemented this training by taking me out in his car. He insisted that I keep a log of the miles that I'd driven, as he wouldn't allow me to drive unaccompanied until I'd logged 1000 miles. He was generous with his time and it didn't take as long as I feared it might (months rather than years).

My dad also wanted to teach me how to drive the boat we had on the lake. I'd driven it a few times, when he thought I could have a go at pulling a water skier. My brother, Charlie, and one of his friends wanted to ski so I went along. Charlie's friend got in the water and my dad made sure he had swum well away from the boat before he turned to show me how to pull away gently until the ski rope was taut. We didn't have a rear-view mirror and we failed to check a final time before we started up. But the boy had panicked, swum back to the boat and been sucked under, into the propeller. The blades had sliced his leg to the bone in three places.

Incredibly, he didn't cry all the way to the hospital, as I tenderly held his leg in a towel. The body shuts down the pain sensors if the trauma would be too great to cope with. I felt hysteria and nausea seething under the surface, which I desperately fought to control for his sake.

I never drove a boat again, nor do I enjoy driving of any sort. Had it not been a vital life skill where we lived, I probably wouldn't have continued to learn to drive a car. Accidents happen in an instant, a momentary lapse and the unthinkable can occur. No reprieve, no opportunity for 'But I didn't mean…'

***

Eventually, we find the hospital and miss the entrance. It's a dual carriageway so I must continue on until I can turn around, drive past on the other side of the barriers, turn around again and hopefully discover the entrance without the fast-moving traffic crashing into us from behind. The car park seems to be randomly plonked at the side of the long driveway. The hospital can be glimpsed in the distance between some trees. At every step, I feel James tense with pain.

We stand for ages at the reception desk. The young woman ignores us and continues what sounds like a social conversation on the phone. When she finishes, I pass the bit of paper we've been given across to her and without looking up she gestures vaguely off to the left.

'Follow the yellow line on the floor.'

More walking. The yellow line runs out. Apart from a cupboard, we appear to have come to a dead end. James is white with fatigue. I try a giggle at the ridiculousness of it all, to lift our spirits. It sounds mad. I wonder if I'm losing my mind.

Someone pops out of the cupboard. There is another long, narrow passage. We come to a small room with very busy people rushing about.

'Your details?' asks a woman sitting behind a computer. She holds her hand out. We stand silently whilst she transfers information to her machine from the bit of paper I give her. We answer her questions and are then sent back to the first desk.

We wait in hard chairs and feel like aliens in this world where we don't know all the words or rules. James is given a test that involves sticking lots of square plasters to his chest and connecting them by wires to a machine.

The technician is cheerful and answers all James' questions. Then we're sent back to the cupboard room for another test.

I want to scream, to tell these people that every step for my son is agony but I don't think they'll hear me. Worse, I don't want my tantrum to turn them against James. It feels like they're just people at work, doing their job in the enormous factory called a hospital. We are the irritating patients (and worse, parents of patients) they have to work around.

At last, we head home feeling completely mangled and despondent, enraged and helpless. I have to do something. I stop at the library and find a book called *Love, Medicine and Miracles* by Dr Bernie Segal. Once home, I start to read. It's full of excellent advice about how to begin to regain some control, to lessen the awful feeling of being a helpless victim.

In the middle of another sleepless night, I get up and write a letter to Dr Edwards. I tell him all about James as a person and how important he is to us. I thank him for his treatment of Howard and James but also outline the appalling events of the day. I feel better for getting these thoughts and feelings down on paper and manage a little sleep.

*

One of my earliest memories was when my family moved out of Detroit to a ranch style house in a much more rural area. At four years old, I was allowed to take my two year old brother, Keith, out to meet some other children, on our own, for the first time. I stood at the edge of the road, tightly clinging to Keith's hand, and looked both ways loads of times before daring to pull him quickly across, despite there being no cars for miles around.

My first friend, Gail, lived just down the road from me and we were inseparable for a few years. I remember the night the nursery-school teacher came to our house to explain to my parents why this best friend, whose birthday was exactly a month before mine and a few days before the admission cut off date, would start proper school a full year before me. I never forgave the woman. As far as I was concerned, it was also her fault when Gail moved away not too long after that. My other memory of nursery school was when my hands stuck to the frozen chains of the playground swing.

I never really had another *best* friend in that neighbourhood. I was always too old or too young for the other girls that lived nearby. By the time my youngest brother, Charlie, was old enough to follow his big brother about like a puppy, it was clear Keith preferred this 'hero-worship' to the bossy meddling of his sister. Despite their endless squabbles, they didn't really want to include me in their games. I used to wade into their disputes and try to protect Charlie, which wasn't appreciated by Keith. He and I always seemed to be arguing and were once sent to another room to 'sort ourselves out' during a meal. Without an audience, we soon ran out of steam.

However, Keith was my brother and *I* was the only one allowed to fight with him. Walking home from school one day, I came across a bully, larger and older than I was, beating Keith up. The anger that exploded in me made me feel about seven feet tall and without hesitation I flew at the brute with my metal lunchbox until he ran off.

It was the early sixties and children's TV was becoming popular but my mother felt that children should be outside and in motion to keep healthy so we were regularly turfed out. I rode my bike, joined in the neighbourhood hide-and-seek, kickball or softball games, climbed trees, rerouted streams, made dens and watched cloud shapes. In winter, gangs of us used to ice skate on the ponds, play hockey, build snowmen and have snowball fights.

But I still spent a lot of time on my own. I found escape in books and expression in writing. Often, I found that getting thoughts down on paper made them more manageable.

***

Back in hospital for the rescheduled tests, we pass Dr Edwards in the corridor. He stops to speak to James and introduces himself to me. He is a great bear of a man, quite overpowering in the narrow space. I am impressed and grateful that he has recognised James, after meeting him only once, and freely offers my son some of his precious time.

'I hadn't expected to see you today, Dr Edwards,' I explain. 'I've written you a letter.' Embarrassed that this isn't quite normal, I hand it to him. I'm further alarmed when he tears it open to read in front of us.

He becomes very still. A male nurse passes us in the corridor and Dr Edwards stops him with a sharp bark. He's furious to discover that the tests he'd ordered haven't been done. I'm sorry for the innocent nurse but hopeful ·that perhaps it won't happen again.

James is taken into theatre. At last things are happening. I can't sit still. My eyes travel over the words on a page but are unable to make sense of the black-and-white shapes. I recognise myself in the faces of other mothers. The new ones, like me, are easy to pick out. We've yet to adjust to the laboriously slow heartbeat of hospital time. We're up and down from our seats and in and out of the toilets.

I meet a mother with very young triplets. One of them has cancer. She smells of smoke and nerves. I think of Edvard Munch's painting of *The Scream*.

Another mother rushes to the sink to wash her hands. I can feel the waves of adrenalin pulsing under her skin. Her eyes are wild with fear. I have a bad habit of studying people. She catches my gaze. Her son is fourteen.

'They say he only has a one in five chance of survival,' she pleads.

'He might be the one who makes it.' Gentle words, given to me, whisper through my lips. 'You can't give up hope.' I touch her arm, longing to steady her. I've thrown her a paper life belt but for a moment it holds and she can catch her breath.

She looks more carefully at me and pauses. 'Yes, I guess that's true.'

We talk. She's on her own. Her doctor husband works abroad so they can afford the private schools they believe their four children need to make it in this world. They are from Nigeria so she may be right. She is a bereavement counsellor, a statement that chokes her as she tells me. Her son, Foluso, has a rare form of kidney cancer. Her name is Agnes. Like me, she is a Christian.

*

I didn't grow up in an overtly religious household. We did go to church sometimes but not regularly. We also prayed at mealtimes but not often. From about age eleven, I begged to stay in the main church rather than go into Sunday school, finding the stories and games silly and childish. I felt grown up being part of the discussions we occasionally had at home afterwards about the sermon.

My clearest memories of church were the fellowship and refreshments that followed and it was something we did as a family. Best of all were the crisp autumn days when we would call into the cider mill on the way home. This was in a faded old barn, framed by crimson leaves. You could watch the massive wheel turn and smell the tang of crushed apple. The sweet, non-alcoholic, cider was perfect with the hot, sugared doughnuts also on offer. *apple juice?*

My grandmothers and both sets of aunts and uncles were Christians, all practising in churches of different denominations. None of these significant adults in my life were preachy or spoke much of their faith to me as a child. Rather, they lived it in my presence.

Despite attending church classes and taking part in a rite of passage in the Presbyterian Church, I still didn't know God in any significant way. Nothing I had been taught seemed particularly relevant to me or revealed the possibility of relationship with God. But perhaps seeds had been sown.

Most summers, I would spend a couple of weeks with my cousin Beth in their log cabin. Aunt Joy and Uncle Glen were both teachers with twelve-week summer holidays. They built their retreat themselves; hidden in the woods on a bay off Lake Michigan. It smelt of pine inside and the sunrise used to make the knots in the logs glow red. We drank cold mint tea made from leaves we'd gathered by the stream.

I was nine months older than Beth, definitely bossier and possibly more confident. Once, I persuaded her to come out further into the lake, on the slippery boulders, than she'd ever been before by giving her a 'magic' pebble that would keep her safe.

My aunt and uncle loved children but, after Beth, had suffered five miscarriages before they had Charlie. One particular day, this precious toddler was standing on a chair at the big table where we shared delicious meals and rowdy games of cards, Monopoly or Scrabble. He was making noisy demands on his mother and Beth and I were ignoring him, intent on our own activities.

Suddenly, for no apparent reason, he fell and began screaming. Even as children ourselves, we recognised that it wasn't a normal baby's cry. My aunt tried desperately to calm him but soon they rushed him off to hospital. Later we learned that he'd had a cerebral aneurysm, which had burst, causing him to fall or because of the fall. Either way there was nothing anyone could have done to prevent the accident.

We were stunned and my cousin distraught. As my aunt and uncle kept a vigil at his bedside, we were left much to ourselves. Desperate to help, I told Beth that maybe, if we were very good, God would let him be OK. I was severely told off for this but didn't fully understand why, then.

My own family had arrived by the time the baby died but nothing in my experience could help me make sense of what was happening. The vision of that tiny white coffin seemed so wrong, so impossible, so unutterably painful.

Not long after that, my other aunt's infant son developed symptoms that seemed to point to hydrocephalus or 'water on the brain'. His surgeon operated before he'd received the results of all the tests, leaving the child blind, retarded and severely epileptic. The tests, when they were consulted, revealed there'd been nothing wrong. These tragedies played at the periphery of my understanding of religion, creating more questions and confusion than comfort. It was to be another tragic event that brought me to faith a few years later.

***

James returns to the ward and this time all the procedures are booked and go to plan but he's very sick from the anaesthetic. He's allowed to come home at the weekend but on Monday we're back for the results.

'The good news is we haven't found cancer anywhere else in James' body but he will need another biopsy. We've booked the surgery for you in Birmingham. They specialise in these paediatric orthopaedic oncology cases. The surgeons there will be able to tell you about possible future options, if your treatment goes to plan.'

"…*if* the treatment goes to plan." Those words reverberate. All these tests and consultations, days and weeks, and now a further delay whilst we go to Birmingham, I just want the treatment to begin.

'Oh, and we discovered James has Wolff-Parkinson-White syndrome. They picked it up when they were doing the baseline tests.'

Words kick the air from my lungs, questions buzz my brain.

'It means there's an extra cluster of nerves that misfire in his heart. Usually, there are no symptoms apart from possibly palpitations. Rarely, it can cause a sudden heart attack or stroke.'

I'm struggling to disentangle the words crashing in my head to form an articulate question. Complications, danger, heart…

'What can we do?' I hear the begging in my voice.

'I think we'll wait and see. It shouldn't be a problem.' The doctor looks away.

Wait and see if he survives the cancer. The completed sentence slides off the doctor's face. I feel sick.

It may be cancer in my family but it's definitely heart disease in Howard's. His father was one of six children, three of them boys. One died of a heart attack in his thirties, another in his fifties. Geoffrey, non-smoking, teetotal, vegetarian and wiry-fit only just made it to sixty.

The drive to Birmingham is a breeze compared to the other things I'm now afraid of. The day is very hot and the nurses are not as approachable as the ones we'd met in the oncology unit in Leeds. It's a big ward with high ceilings and tall windows glaring with July sunlight. The room is full of children, babies through teens, and their families. We're told the boy in the next bed, who is on his own and curled beneath a sheet, had come in the previous Tuesday for tests and they'd taken his leg off on Wednesday. There is no TV to distract the children and it's very noisy. James is in a lot of pain and frightened, particularly about facing another anaesthetic.

Thankfully, the anaesthetist comes to see him in the evening and she is lovely. She tells him she will use a new gas, which is very expensive and also agrees to try the 'power of suggestion' techniques I'd read about.

The surgeons also come to see James to explain the possible surgical options that will be considered, in October, when he will return once the chemotherapy has begun its work. The cancerous section of bone can be removed, when enough of the cells are dead, and a metal replacement fitted. They tell us that cancer surgery is highly specialised and that cancer cells would have been spilled into the wound during his previous operation so even the scar tissue on the front of his leg will have to be removed.

He is given a pre-med, which makes him sleep all day, and it works, he isn't sick at all. The biopsy goes smoothly and Howard is able to rush tissue samples back to Leeds on Wednesday night so that their lab and the lab in Birmingham can work on them simultaneously.

When James wakes from the surgery, he finds the spot where his groin biopsy had been done the previous week has swelled to the size of an egg. He's terrified. We ask a junior doctor about it.

'Oh dear, it wasn't like that yesterday. I've no idea what the problem is.' The young man shakes his head and walks off.

I don't know what to say to James.

When a nurse comes to take the crepe bandage off, the cotton wool underneath is covered in blood. Horrified, James cries out, 'Oh no, the cancer cells will be all round my leg now!'

The nurse makes a peculiar face and goes away. It doesn't feel much like the team work Dr Edwards had described to Howard.

James and I have to stay an extra day, as James needs an additional test but is too sleepy to drink the radioactive contrasts needed to highlight problems undetectable by more ordinary methods. We are sent to yet another hospital in Birmingham, by taxi so at least I don't have the anxiety of driving.

After a 45-minute wait, a man appears and says, 'Where are your notes?' The notes are then dispatched in another taxi and we wait 45 minutes more. I'm furious at being made to feel stupid for not bringing the notes, when I'm simply a complete novice to the whole system. (James' notes apparently don't specify that he needs to drink contrasts so he will have to have the test done again, a week and a half later in Leeds.)

By this time James is long overdue for his painkillers and is in some distress. It's difficult to describe what it feels like to witness your child in agony and be unable to do anything about it. Imagine every muscle pulsing with angry bees and their buzzing filling your mind. I ask a passing nurse if James can be given something for his pain.

'I'll see what I can do,' she says. She smiles then proceeds to walk across the room where she stops and talks to a friend about her holidays. She doesn't bother to lower her voice. Their laughter fills the space between us. She doesn't return. The buzzing gets louder. My hands ball into fists.

The hospital pharmacy won't sell me anything over the counter so in desperation I leave James and go in search of a chemist. The people I ask for directions step back in alarm. I must look wild. I'm slick with sweat when I return with the Ibuprofen.

The nurses in Birmingham don't like to use portacaths so, despite having a needle in already, they insisted on putting another needle into James' hand. This then has to be removed before we will be allowed to go home. The nurse is busy and asks us to wait. After forty-five minutes (a magic number in Birmingham?) I suspect she's forgotten us. I ask her again, and finally we're on our way.

James is quiet, always a bad sign, and tries to disappear into the music on his walkman. My skin feels too small and tight to contain the thoughts and feelings swarming inside.

*

Animal-mad as a child, I almost always had a pet of some description, usually adopted waifs and strays. Often they were either rescued, like the baby wild rabbits I'd found when their mother was killed by a dog, or captured like my collection of grass snakes. I'd been given a puppy one Christmas, when I was six, but he'd been returned to Santa when he resisted all attempts at house training.

I was forever getting involved with animals I should have stayed away from. Once when bitten by a stray dog, I had to travel the neighbourhood in a police car to try to find it, in case it had rabies. I was strictly forbidden to touch wild animals so I didn't tell my parents when the field mouse I'd caught bit me. Miraculously, I escaped unscathed when I waded into a dogfight to split up the combatants but wasn't so lucky when I tried to feed a pet monkey tied up in someone's garden.

My all-consuming passion was for horses. From age eight it was all I ever asked for when it was my birthday or Christmas and I saved every penny I was ever given, found or earned. When I was thirteen, I came to an agreement with my parents that I would do all the housework in exchange for the cost of renting a fat old horse called Missy, from a girl that was going off to university but couldn't bear to sell her.

Eventually, at fifteen, I bought a two year old, unbroken appaloosa horse with huge ears. Spook was very cheap. I think my record was being thrown off twelve times in one day but, gradually, I trained her and she became a lovely, gentle companion.

I had several part time jobs in order to pay Spook's board and save for university, including the housework at home, bookkeeping for my dad's company, regular babysitting, a Saturday job in a chemist and exercising two polo ponies. I also worked off some of the cost of keeping my horse by feeding all the other horses and cleaning the stables.

I began to learn the patience I would need as a teacher and a mother, especially the mother of a seriously-ill child.

***

Back in Leeds, we're told that James' cancer, like many of the cancers that affect teenagers, is very unusual. It's a desmoplastic small round cell tumour, which is closely related to pPNET/Ewings but hasn't been recognised in bone before. Thankfully, no cancer has been found anywhere else yet, always a great fear with this disease, as it then becomes much harder to treat and contain.

His treatment will be fourteen cycles of chemotherapy, assessment of response after the second and fourth cycles, with surgery just prior to the fifth, assuming a good response. He will be given the drugs intravenously from Tuesday lunchtime until Friday evening, followed by two weeks off to recover. The possible side effects come in three categories:

- ☐ Acute visible – hair loss, nausea/sickness, nutrition/weight loss, constipation

- ☐ Invisible – bone marrow suppression leading to anaemia, infections and bruising

- ☐ Long term – infertility, second tumour, heart function, kidney problems

James qualifies for participation in a clinical study for which he will receive 10 daily injections, between the chemotherapy cycles, of a drug called Granulocyte Colony Stimulating Factor (GCSF), which stimulates the production of white cells and can reduce the risk of infections by 50%. He has to learn to give these injections himself.

My aunt telephones. She's a doctor and for a time worked for the United States government in Washington DC.

'I've been praying for you all, every day,' she tells me. 'Last night I woke up, knowing I had to phone a past colleague of mine. When I reached him, he gave me the number of a doctor who works for the National Cancer Research Centre. I've spoken to her and she has suggested you phone her. She wants to help, if she can.'

My heart leaps to think that God is answering prayers about James.

I telephone this woman and she's lovely. She tells me about a food supplement called Coenzyme Q10. There has been some positive research that appears to show it can help to protect the heart and other organs from the effects of chemotherapy. I check with Dr Edwards, who doesn't think it can do any harm, and start James on them immediately.

*

Whilst we'd been at the hospital for all the earlier tests on James, I'd taken this same aunt's advice to enter a regular mammogram-screening program. She was my mother's only sister and had both breasts removed with cancer. My maternal grandmother, great aunt and grandfather had also suffered from various forms of the disease.

Having squashed my delicate bits into this ruthless machine, the technician took several 'plates' and went away. She came back after a while and took some more, then returned to inform me that I'd had the maximum dose of radiation for the day. She asked me to come back for some more pictures the following week.

Trying not to worry, I carried on until my next appointment. After examining yet more 'plates' I was told there was an abnormality and I would be referred to a specialist. It was as if the sound of the woman's voice was going into someone else's ears, the same person who was operating my arms and legs for me. I went on from there to the supermarket and, as I walked through the door, I burst into tears.

The specialist used ultrasound, which was a great deal less painful than the mammogram, and declared that what I had was a harmless, flat cist. I suggested it had probably been round before they flattened it in their machine. I had to return in six weeks to be certain that it was nothing to worry about and was then given the all-clear. They told me my badminton muscles made it hard for them to get good pictures but I blame that machine, which was obviously invented by a man with limited understanding of female anatomy.

***

We are determined that at the end of all this we won't have to be haunted by 'what if's. We try to investigate every possible way to help James; items brought to our attention by family or friends, information found on the Internet, in newspapers, magazines or books. We attempt to double-check anything we find to ensure whatever decisions we have to make are as well informed as possible.

Fast or pre-packaged foods are discarded in favour of lots of fresh fruit and vegetables and home-made meals. I take James swimming because it's an exercise he can do without pain. I encourage him to try visual imaging. This is when you visualise your immune system to be made up of strong and powerful creatures, which attack the horrible cancer cells. We go to funny films, share jokes and watch things that make us laugh on TV because laughter releases endorphins to boost the immune system. We claw back some control over the situation.

Perhaps because of his age and the very real risk of infertility, the doctors offer James the opportunity to have some of his sperm frozen before his treatment begins. He finds this excruciatingly embarrassing. But James is determined that he will get well and wants at least to have the opportunity to lead a normal life so he perseveres until the mission is accomplised.

Adjusting to being pushed in a wheelchair is another experience that takes courage. James says he can't believe the difference in the way people look at him when in a wheelchair compared to when he's managing on crutches. But a wheelchair enables him to get out more, as walking on crutches is quite exhausting to say nothing of coping with the increasing pain. To all critics of shopping malls, I would suggest they try to push an adult in a wheelchair. Certainly in our local town, if not most towns, broken pavements, curbs and doorsills often make it impossible.

*

The phone call from my mother's sister and the thought of my son being a parent some day makes me think about my mom. We were opposites in many ways, which made understanding one another challenging at times. I was a 'homebody' and didn't mind being on my own where Mom thrived on the company of others. She'd been a 'daddy's girl' and didn't always see eye to eye with her mom. My dad worked and played hard, wasn't very affectionate and, as a child, I found him a bit aloof. I knew he loved me and was proud of me. There were tickling games when we were little and I remember my first time skiing down a slope in the awesome Rocky Mountains between the protective 'v' of his skis. But I longed to be a 'mommy's girl'.

I remember feeling a mixture of guilt, pride and excitement as a little girl, when my mother took me out of school early on Wednesdays to learn to ski. She was a high school PE teacher then and ran a ski club. Judging by the amount of time I spent sitting behind the class piano for talking, I imagine my teacher was relieved to see me go.

From a young age, Mom tried to instil in us a love of music. I can vividly remember, dancing round the living room to the powerful notes of Grieg's 'In the Hall of the Mountain King'. She enjoyed a wide range of genres but I always think about her when I hear 'Climb Every Mountain' from *The Sound of Music* or 'To Dream the Impossible Dream' from *Man from La Mancha*.

Once when I'd broken the rules and stayed out after dark, losing track of time in the excitement of a neighbourhood game, my mother told me she would have to spank me. We had a wooden paddle that was a souvenir from a fraternity or sorority house. She said it was the only way she could think of to make me realise the importance of being home on time and respecting rules. There were tears in her eyes when she'd done it and they hurt a lot more than the tap on my bottom.

When my mother decided to go back to university to do a Master's and PhD in clinical psychology, she continued to work part-time and remained active in her sport and social activities. I was very jealous and disappointed when my brothers were able to go off on various 'boys only' events with my dad but the promised 'girls days out' never materialised.

As busy as my mother was, for a few years we had a wonderful woman called Bertha who looked after us a few days a week and tried to keep the house clean. She was originally from Mexico and introduced us to a new culture and delicious foods. For a time, my youngest brother knew more Spanish words than English.

One day, when I'd brought a friend home from school, I found my mom and Bertha enjoying a cup of coffee together in the kitchen. I proceeded to introduce them to my friend saying, 'This is my mom and Bertha, our cleaning lady.' There was a horrified silence and I was subsequently informed that I had done a gross unkindness to Bertha in not introducing her as 'our friend'. It hadn't occurred to me that cleaning ladies weren't also, obviously, friends.

My mother encouraged me to believe in myself. One summer I had the idea of setting up a sort of day camp for younger children from the neighbourhood, in our garden. I must have been about twelve. She listened to my enthusiasm and gently added questions that would help me to think it through more carefully and make it a success. I went door to door asking the parents, planned outings we could do on foot, got cookies and juice ready, played games and read stories, all good practice for the teaching I would do later in life.

The long twelve-week holidays were a struggle for working parents. I resisted organised groups like summer camps but I was often sent to spend a fortnight with either my cousin in the log cabin in Northern Michigan or my cousins in Maryland. My brothers never seemed to do this, although they also had male cousins of similar ages, and neither did any of my cousins ever come to stay with us.

Perhaps because of this I developed quite overwhelming homesickness, which was treated as silly nonsense. It wasn't so bad during the day, when I could keep busy, but alone at night it engulfed me. When my crying disturbed my cousins in Maryland, after trying unsuccessfully to soothe me, I was made to sleep in my uncle's office attached to the house and eventually given something to help me sleep. At sixth grade school camp, I cried so much I was ill and they sent me home. My mother promptly sent me back the next day.

In my pre- and early teen years, my mom would sometimes come and lie beside me at bedtime and we would talk. She discussed in general terms the kinds of problems some of the children in her care were facing and the ways in which she tried to help them unlock their fears and pain. She taught me that loud show-offs were often the most insecure and made me wonder at the idea that you need to love yourself before others can love you.

I felt grown up and privileged to be able to share in her experiences and felt secure enough to talk to her about my most secret discoveries, personal trials and tribulations. Away from distractions, what we lacked in quantity of time together, we made up for in quality.

Chapter 2

Tuesday 23 July 1996

James has his first dose of chemotherapy, today, at last. He's frightened, twitchy and unable to take his eyes from the tube, as he watches the toxic orange chemicals travel down from the bag into his body. It makes him feel very tired and he sleeps most of the day. On Wednesday night, he starts to vomit and carries on all through the next day. I fetch endless cardboard bowls, stroke his clammy skin and beg nurses and doctors to do something. Finally, heavily sedated he collapses into a deep sleep on Thursday night, beginning to be sick again Friday morning.

By Saturday, he's able to keep fluids down so they let him come home. Unfortunately, he's severely constipated (he hadn't 'been' for three weeks) and by Sunday he starts vomiting again.

It's late but our GP comes out to our house and tries to help him 'go' for about an hour until James collapses from exhaustion.

'His pulse is stable,' this kind man says. His youngest son went to nursery school with James. 'He's asleep now. I'll come back in the morning.' I can see desperation in his eyes.

James wakes an hour later and begins to be sick again. This time he brings up blood so we rush him back to the hospital at 2am, breaking a few speed limits on the way. Thankfully, my dad and his wife, Lynda, have come over to help so are able to stay with David.

James looks like we've snatched him from a concentration camp. He's lost a stone (6+ kg) in weight from his previously slim frame. His skin is grey with hollow cheeks and black sunken eyes. The doctor, who staggers sleepily in to see us, looks too young. She tells us that James is badly dehydrated and very low on potassium. James is hooked up to a drip and by morning is much improved. It takes the greater part of the week to clear the backlog and get his system back into something like working order.

Being young and relatively fit before all this began, and possibly due to the GCSF and the Coenzyme Q10, James bounces back quite quickly. Much of his pain seems to go with the first chemotherapy and the tumour, which is now a very visible swelling on his lower leg, begins to shrink. He puts some weight back on and goes swimming most days to keep his strength up. He begins to lose his hair and asks his dad to shave it off. Seeing James ·without his thick, wavy, dark hair isn't so bad but the missing eyebrows and eyelashes take some getting used to.

We begin to appreciate the wonderful team of people working on the children's and teenage cancer wards. We're visited by dieticians who provide us with supplements (like Build-up to maximise the calories and vitamins James can take in when well enough to eat), social workers to support the whole family (helping with benefits, sibling clubs, etc), physiotherapists, a liaison nurse to coordinate between all the services (organising a wheel chair, communicating with the school and GP), play coordinators (providing games, videos and the Jolly Trolley full of sweets), teachers to help the children keep up with their school work, psychologists, nurses, porters, cleaners and not least the doctors and consultants. The Macmillan nurse sits quietly beside me, unrushed amidst the hustle of the ward, and lets me talk out all my fears and concerns, bringing huge relief by just listening.

The paediatric oncology unit is part of a university hospital so quite a few of those responsible for James' care are students and, along with the other more experienced people, they can and do make mistakes. So far in the course of his treatment, we've been to six different hospitals. We begin to realise how important our role in James' care is. We are the one constant throughout the process. I begin to keep a ring binder full of the notes we take, information given to us from various bodies, drug schedules, phone numbers, maps and anything else that seems significant. It's a tiny measure of control, a step away from victimhood.

*

In September 1985, James started 'big' school. I should have been thrilled at the way he skipped off for his first day without looking back once. After all, we wanted him to be a confident, happy, independent person. And part of me was glad for him, but a big part was heartbroken that he didn't seem to need me anymore. I could feel tears welling up.

Suddenly, our very wise doctor's wife invited all the new mums to her house for a Tupperware party. She'd just seen her third and youngest child enter the next phase of his life and understood what we were feeling.

The thrill of meeting James, with open arms, at the end of that day and listening to his excitement was tremendous. I was still needed, it was only the role I was allowed to play that had changed.

School and its attendant germs resulted in James developing rather a lot of chest and throat infections. There are some things you pray your children won't inherit but it seemed we shared a susceptibility to tonsillitis. Our doctor told us he had something called 'exertional wheeze' and gave him a spinhalor. Increasingly it became apparent that this wasn't enough and the doctor put him on the waiting list to have his tonsils out.

Just before Christmas, James was called for his tonsillectomy. I was terrified. When I was thirteen and new to the neighbourhood, I had been shown the house where a boy had died having his tonsils out. I couldn't escape from that haunting memory.

I tried to put a brave face on for my son. We read, talked and played until they anaesthetised and wheeled him away into theatre. I waited in the overly heated room, too anxious to eat, with the parents of three little girls, also in surgery for their tonsils. The girls all returned to their beds, awake and vomiting but safe. Time ticked by and no James arrived. When finally he returned to his bed, he was still unconscious. My fear mounted with each passing moment. At last, just as his eyes fluttered open, I was completely overcome with relief and passed out.

I discovered, once I'd recovered from my embarrassment, that the girls had been given different drugs to James so had responded differently. My son wasn't sick like the others but he did develop an infection, which left him unable to eat without pain or sleep through the night for ten days. Whilst the operation did reduce the number of throat infections and antibiotics James had to have, it didn't solve the fact that he had mild asthma and rhinitis and needed to use an inhaler throughout his childhood.

***

We are overwhelmed with gratitude for the response of our friends and family. It truly is the love of God in action. People think of small gifts, kindnesses and practical, useful things, which amaze us. James makes a collection of all the cards and postcards he receives and covers his bedroom wall with them.

My Aunt Joy sends me a small, spiral 'thought for the day' book. I stand it on a shelf in the Welsh dresser and flip it over each morning. It's one of the comforting routines I cling to. I'm amazed by how often it seems to speak directly into whatever situation I find myself in. One morning, it stops me in my tracks. The reading is from 1 Thessalonians 5.15-18, *Be joyful always; pray continually; give thanks in all circumstances, for this is God's will for you in Christ Jesus.*

I can *not* be thankful that James is so ill. For days I feel defensive and confused. My brain can't let it go. I talk to people, pray and worry at the puzzle like a demented terrier. Gradually, I begin to understand that it means I should look for something to be thankful for within every circumstance not necessarily for the circumstance itself. It becomes a challenge for me to seek out, each day, things I can thank God for. And it does help. There is power in choosing how you respond to a situation. The principle is the same as 'counting your blessings', finding the 'silver lining' in a black cloud or looking at the glass as 'half-full' instead of 'half-empty'.

We spend part of every evening on the phone, as friends let us know we're in their thoughts and prayers. I welcome the opportunity to talk but know some families who tape an update on their child's progress straight onto their answering machines, when they can't face re-living the day.

David has a holiday with the scouts, to Wales, which is a very important break for him. He has a wonderful time and we're grateful to the sensitive leaders and other boys who help him to escape the ordeal at home. He looks even taller, when he gets back, tanned, fit and healthy. He's been swimming every day, walking, playing sport and riding quad bikes.

'We played a game where we had to swim out deep in the sea, take our trunks off, whirl them around our heads then race to see who could get them back on the quickest.' David blushes with the memory. 'I always won,' he claims.

'We even went to the pub one night,' he grins and pauses to watch our reaction to this, 'but I only had lemonade.'

'I saw my first adder,' he boasts and brushes off my alarm.

'The younger scouts were very annoying.' He pulls himself up to his full height and saunters off to tell his friends about his adventures.

*

I remember when David was born. I woke up feeling strange tightening sensations around my huge bump. This was, of course, the one day when Howard would not be in his usual office and very difficult to reach. It was two and a half weeks before my due date but I began to suspect that this baby might decide to emulate its brother and make an early appearance. I asked Howard to phone periodically during the day, as this could be 'it'. He said he would but I could tell he was hoping this was just another pregnant woman's fancy.

I alerted my wonderful, elderly neighbours, who were very excited and started making contingency plans immediately. Then the 'nesting' instinct took hold and I cleaned the house with fervour. The tightening sensations gradually increased in frequency and strength throughout the day.

In the evening, Howard's eighteen-year-old brother, Matthew, kindly came over to spend the night, as cover for James in case we had to go to the hospital. Then the pains just stopped, at about 11pm, and I went to bed feeling slightly disappointed. They started again with a vengeance around 5:30 am and we were able to get up, without a fuss, fully prepared and go to the hospital.

This experience was so completely different to my first delivery it was almost unrecognisable as the same event. There was time for all the usual preparations, even breakfast had I wanted it (who were they kidding?). Howard gratefully enjoyed the bacon and eggs they brought for me. I had been to the antenatal classes this time and knew that movement would actually help. My attentive husband rubbed my aching back and kept me company until my beautiful baby boy made his welcome appearance about 9:30am. Remarkably, David has continued to be as easy and thoughtful throughout his life.

David had been born in an old fashioned maternity hospital with big windows and pleasant companions. I was almost sorry I hadn't opted for a longer stay to catch up on some rest and get to know this new little mite. In a quiet moment I was filled with wonder at the gift God had given me in the safe arrival of this precious, healthy child.

Later in the day when Howard went home to collect James, he was surprised to find James' shirt was wet all around the bottom edge. Apparently, Matthew had tried to change a disgustingly dirty nappy and in the end had decided the only solution was to put him in the bath. However, as James cried when he tried to take off his shirt, Matthew had decided to leave it on.

When Howard and James arrived to take me home, I was staggered to see the size of my eldest son. He had been my little baby the day before but now, next to David, he looked like a giant. How would he react, at only twenty months old, to sharing his parents with a little brother? Thankfully, apart from a major hiccup in his potty training, there didn't seem to be any real problems on that front.

When we'd brought James home from hospital, Howard's mum explained that she'd always started her babies off in their own rooms because otherwise you would have to wean them from sharing your room at some point and it would get harder the longer you left it.

That seemed to make sense, she did have rather a lot of experience with her own six babies, but I was worried that I wouldn't hear him cry. After all, I once slept through a fire alarm in the dormitories at university. I needn't have bothered. It is one of the many miracles of motherhood that no matter how tired I was, and breast-feeding mothers get extremely tired, I always woke whenever either of them cried.

With James, I used to talk, sing or tell him stories the whole time I was feeding him but with David, I would just doze in the comfy quiet as he suckled. I was either so much more relaxed or so much more exhausted. It's interesting that James has always been a boisterous, chatty person whilst David is much quieter and more reserved. We loved them both the same and they grew up in the same environment yet it always amazes us how different they are.

***

Just in case we're tempted to think we have enough on our minds, Howard's company is sold. On the Monday before James' second chemotherapy; Howard has to endure a three-hour interview with the new directors, presumably to decide if they want to keep him. Howard feels that their response has been positive and his job is probably safe, but there will be a lot of changes, additional pressure, stress and insecurity. He is keenly aware that he won't be able to put everything into making a good impression, given our situation, and worries about being passed over or demoted.

On the positive side, we're able to cash in some of our share options, reducing our mortgage and overheads, which will relieve possible future financial pressures should I have to stay off work beyond the time I am eligible for full pay.

The petrol needed to drive James to hospitals as far as Birmingham and to visit him whilst he's there, does not come cheap, to say nothing of car parking charges. The worries a family faces when a member is seriously ill are many and complex. Sadly, financial difficulties often add layers to the distress.

Discreetly and separately, I am approached by members of two different families in our church. They offer whatever financial assistance we may need. Churches are full of flawed human beings who make mistakes and get things wrong but my heart almost bursts with wonder at God's love in action through the body of this church.

*

Finances were also one of the practical problems to be solved before Howard and I could get married. In England on a student visa for six months, ·with only two months left after my teaching practice, I was not allowed to work without a permit. I had no money and no place to stay, without adding further financial burden to Howard's family. Howard still had a year and a bit of college to complete. We didn't want to feel we were being forced into marriage and I wanted to be sure I could live away from my family.

Howard's parents had both left school in their mid-teens, as was usual for their day, but unusually had taken on a mortgage and bought the largest house they could possibly afford. This turned out to be an inspired decision in later years. They were both extremely hard working; he turned his hand to various jobs including salesman, postman and progress chaser and she was a mender in a local mill, continuing the work from home when her children were small. They took the problem of another mouth to feed in their stride and made me feel part of the family but I was anxious to contribute.

To get a work permit at that time you needed a job, as the employer applied for the permit, but you couldn't get a job without a permit – classic Catch 22. You also needed to prove that there were no English people available to do the job. I managed to get a position with a Pakistani family, as a nanny. They had advertised for a year without success. The mother was a midwife who worked twelve-hour night shifts and the father had only just lost his job but was actively searching for another. So keen were they to get someone to care for the children that they were prepared to apply for my permit and let me work for them whilst we awaited the results.

It was perfect. It provided me with a place to stay and a small income. The family were lovely with a little girl of four and a boy, two. I tried to keep the children out in the park or swimming during the morning to allow their mother to get some sleep but without fail she would be up working in her house when we got back for lunch. I don't know how she could keep up such a pace.

I shared many a good-natured discussion with the father about the advantages of arranged marriage verses the western approach. I never could convince him and he was appalled that I was planning to marry someone my dad had never even met. Still, they welcomed Howard into their home, when he came to visit, and even fixed a meal for us.

After three months the application for the permit was turned down and I had to move back to Howard's parents' home. I had been a regular visitor over the previous months and got on very well with his parents and siblings. He was the second of six children. They were a very lively, musical family and had even been on TV in *Stars on Sunday.*

I loved the hustle and bustle as everyone got ready to walk to church and the sound and feel of the music there. The church itself gave me the sensation of a large, comfy grandma embracing me to her bosom. Coming from a place where families seemed to spread across the country like dice on a gaming table, I was attracted to the stability and closeness of this family, who had been part of the same community for generations and who welcomed me without question.

Quite quickly, I secured another job, with a Church of England Children's Home. They'd also had the position advertised for twelve months without success, as they wanted someone with childcare qualifications that was prepared to live in. But they weren't able to let me start until the permit came through.

In the meantime, I tried to make myself useful to Howard's family, helping with the housework, cooking, watching his youngest brother's football games. Howard was back at college for some of this time and also working for a man he'd worked for since he was thirteen, fitting tyres and exhausts. To help fill my time, I made Howard a silver grey suit, from locally produced wool, to get married in. It was my first attempt at a suit and it is a measure of his love for me that he actually wore it at our wedding.

Howard's younger sister, Lorraine, arranged for me to do a few hours of work at the bakery where she had a Saturday job, which earned me a few more pennies. I also helped voluntarily on the church's Thursday coffee morning rota.   — pouring hot water .

This was a great service to the local community, especially its elderly members. It was market day in the small town and the church opened its schoolrooms, selling coffee and biscuits at a very affordable price. Because it wasn't a commercial enterprise people were allowed to stay as long as they wished, providing a warm, safe, social outlet for many single and/or isolated people. We also took hot coffee out to the frozen market traders.

During the three months following the end of my post as nanny, we were busy trying to get the necessary paperwork in place to enable me to stay in England until Howard finished his course. The local MP appealed on our behalf and we even travelled to London during the Silver Jubilee to speak to people at the Home Office, in person. However, it was all in vain. In October, I received notification that I had two weeks to leave the country. My student visa had expired and I was deported.

***

As James begins his second round of chemotherapy, a boy with Down's syndrome is in the next bed. He's cared for by a foster family. As well as leukaemia, he just has one arm. But there is only ever laughter in their corner of the room. Nurses come from other wards just to chat with these remarkable people. The boy and his parents move among the other families and ask after our children. Their hopefulness and love lighten the day.

James is given a cocktail of anti-sickness drugs this time. I've bought him an acupuncture wrist band, for people who suffer seasickness, to try as well. It's not meant to be worn for long periods of time, though, and rubs his wrist raw. Thankfully, the drugs work and although he feels dizzy, nauseous and thoroughly rotten, he isn't sick. This means he's able to come home on Friday night and bounces back much more quickly.

However, his leg is beginning to hurt again and it's clear that the tumour is getting bigger. We tell ourselves it's just fluid and measure the circumference of his leg every day but there is no denying that the chemotherapy isn't enough.

I wait for James outside the clinic in the sunshine. He's gone to the toilet before the long drive home. The cloying smells from the over-warm waiting room upstairs cling to my clothes and clog my throat.

There's a father and daughter, Clair, outside waiting for her mum to pick them up in their car. Clair is seventeen and has been in hospital almost without a break for a year. She's had cancer in several places in her body. Hope glows from her smile. The cancerous bone in her leg has been replaced with a metal substitute and she can walk again. Her wheelchair, with pink go-faster stripes is home in the garage. She giggles and tells me she's learning to drive.

Her father listens to my account of James. Parents learn to share these horrors with each other. We understand. We are united in this war against cancer. There can be comfort in numbers. *Discussion on presence of Claire*

'Before this,' he gestures to encompass the clinic and the hospital, 'I never would have believed how many different ways there are to be terrified.'

We swap news of other families. I'm heartbroken to hear the mum with the triplets has had a nervous breakdown. I ask if they know anything about a tiny baby I often noticed on its own in a side room.

The father looks away before he explains. The parents of the infant are very young. There is no hope. They can't cope.

I realise that I will be no good to anyone if I don't make some effort to look after myself. So even though it's like forcing sawdust down my throat, I make myself eat and although I would rather stay in James' hospital bed in his place, I make myself go home at night to sleep and at least see David. I also decide to take my doctor's advice and accept extended sick leave from work.

There is some guilt attached to this decision. James is determined to go to school as often as he can. We support this and believe the normality is important and his friends are vital. He's in the second year of his GCSE studies. The grades he earns in the exams at the end of this school year will determine where or if he will go to university. The work gives him something to focus on, a goal to strive for.

To teach very young children you have to be 100% and I'm clearly not that. But if I went into work when James was at school and only took days off when he wasn't well enough or needed to go to the hospital, my school would ·have to wait until I was off for a day each time before the insurance would pay for a supply teacher for my class. This would be very disruptive, as the head teacher would have to stand in or my children split up and distributed amongst the other classes. There would be no guarantee of having the same supply teacher each time, either. The children and my colleagues would suffer and I would feel responsible. But I also feel guilty when I'm at home and James is in school. To try to assuage the guilt, I spend some of the time making teaching resources for my colleagues.

The awesome power of 'church' strengthens me. On Sundays, week by week, the congregation prays for James and often the music releases the tears I try to hide from my family. We receive a card from a prayer team in Pennsylvania. They are praying for us, which is amazing because we don't know anyone who lives in that state. Family and friends from around the world report that prayers are said for James in their churches, too. But I am struggling to pray.

*

Nine days after my fourteenth birthday, I kissed my mother goodnight, as usual, and never saw her again.

I was the 'new girl' in school. We'd moved into the area four months previously and I struggled to make friends. News leaked out that I had skipped a school year and many thought I must be a freak. Tall and scrawny with 'mad professor' hair, I never quite fit into any of life's 'little boxes'. Athletic but also academic, I loved animals, writing and art. Self-conscious about my height, I always wished to be a petite, pretty girl who would be easy to cuddle instead of the spiky, gangling tomboy that I was.

One girl befriended me but I later learned that she was very disturbed. She self mutilated and was pregnant by the age of fifteen. It became apparent that she'd spread nasty stories about me so that I would be dependant on her for friendship. I caught her showing private letters of mine, relating details of a current crush, to people on the school bus. To my shame, we fought in front of everyone.

My mom had persuaded me to invite another girl home, in an effort to help me build some new friendships.

The road was dry and clear for a January afternoon. We walked to my house from the bus, having said little on the journey amongst the jungle noise of teenagers escaping school. My mind had that chill-cabinet sluggishness and the fear of saying something stupid paralysed my tongue.

'Wasn't Mr Richards weird today?' I ventured, as the throbbing silence pressed.

'Yeah,' Melanie said.

'Are you hungry?' I asked.

'Yeah, are you?'

'Starving, we should be able to find something at home.' Our footsteps scuffed against the tarmac. 'It isn't far.'

Melanie glanced round. She looked as unsure of what we were doing as I felt.

Seeing an unfamiliar car on the drive sent the first ice critters skittering round my stomach. My aunt and uncle were waiting inside the house. The look on my aunt's face sucked the air from my lungs and I scrabbled to sit down. I heard her voice muffled through miles of fog.

'Your mother's been in an accident.'

'But she's going to be OK, right?' A tiny voice came from my mechanically moving lips.

'It's very serious. She's in a coma and your Dad's at the hospital with her now.' My aunt's voice ached in the telling of this news and blew sour fear in my face.

Over time we learned that my two brothers had missed their school bus that morning. As I was older and in high school, I always left at 6:30 am, before the rest of the family was awake. The extra journey had made my mother late for work and she carelessly rushed through an often misleading railway stoplight, on a blind corner. A fairly slow-moving train had hit Mom's car, causing her lunchtime tin of soup on the passenger seat to fly up and crack her in the head.

I don't know what happened to the poor girl that had come home with me. Sitting in the hospital waiting room, my brothers and I were silent. We daren't look at one another for fear of seeing our worst nightmares mirrored in each other's eyes. Outrage, that I wouldn't be allowed to visit my mother because I was too young, mixed with a kind of relief that I wouldn't have to see her bruised and helpless when I most craved her strength. But I have spent my life wondering if the sounds of our voices or the sensation of our hugs could have called her back to us.

My brothers and I spent the next week at my aunt and uncle's house. I felt like a jigsaw with all the pieces pushed into the wrong places and had the curious experience of looking out at the world and seeing it in negative. There was an unnatural quiet, even my young cousins sensed the black fear that had moved in with us.

It was then felt that we needed some semblance of 'normality' back in our lives so we were sent to school the second week. If I'd felt a freak before, it was nothing to the silence or stilted speech that followed me everywhere and did little to ease the hypersensitivity through which I sieved every utterance. At least at school I could focus my mind on the work, escaping my feelings. It was the nights alone in the dark, when my heart would race and unformed fears would press down on my skull. The possibility of life without my mother was an unknown that made all else pale into insignificance.

We had only lived in our new house for nine days, when the accident happened. We'd been in rented accommodation for four months previously so that we children could start the school year in our new classes. It was a beautiful house, my parent's dream, but never achieved that feeling of home I'd known in the place I'd grown up. It was built into a hillside so that from the front it looked like a bungalow but on the lakeside the lower level revealed itself through large glass sliding doors. Unfortunately, in the midst of our troubles, the whole of this level flooded, ruining all the new carpets and causing the freshly stocked chest freezer to fail. In addition to this, some people who had been involved in a minor bump a few years earlier decided it would be a good time to sue my mother whilst she was unconscious. There was a tension among us, wondering what the next blow would be.

My dad worked all hours to establish his fledgling business and spent as much time as possible with my mom. He looked haunted when I did see him, which wasn't often. My brothers were on stunned autopilot, in as much need as I was. My grandmothers, who had full and active lives themselves, struggled to take it in turns to help us out and were also shattered that this was happening to their children. I had no friends to turn to. In the darkness, and in desperation, I talked to God.

Perhaps because I came to Him as a child, or because the depth of my need had stripped me of any illusion that I could cope with this loss on my own, I began to pray. I begged. I pleaded. I even tried to make bargains with God. I promised to stop fighting with my brothers, to always be good, to pray every day.

As the weeks went on though, my mother didn't seem to improve. At first we'd been given a 20% chance, which to a child meant hope. Gradually and gently my grandmother, who was a nurse, made it clear that if Mom did survive, she would in all probability be brain damaged, a vegetable.

I couldn't imagine a worse fate for a woman as beautiful, clever and active as my mother, someone who despised self-pity and dreaded being old or infirm. She was 37 years old, the loving mother of three young children, had been studying for a PhD, worked as a clinical psychologist, was the State's golf champion, skied, played bridge, bowled regularly and enjoyed a very full social life.

As the reality of the situation became clearer for me, I didn't know what to pray for. I couldn't bear to be without her yet couldn't ask that she survive at *any* cost. Finally, I went to God and put all my trust in Him. I prayed that His will be done; it was far too enormous for me. A kind of peace smoothed the brittle spikes in my chest. I felt released from any responsibility. I suddenly knew that I would never be alone whilst I had God and he would help me face whatever was to come.

When I was little, my brothers and I used to play a game where we had to stand at the end of the bed, close our eyes and fall backwards, without bending our knees. We knew in our minds that the bed was there and that it would be safe but our bodies had no sensory confirmation and had to trust in the mind's message. Like a fairground ride, it was fun to be able to feel fear in safety.

I could learn about God from the Bible, church or the stories of others but I needed to have faith before I could feel His presence, before He became real for me. When I prayed 'Your will be done', it was as if I'd closed my eyes to all that I 'knew' about the world and fell back into the arms of God.

That revelation didn't mean my life would be pain free, that I would be cocooned in some kind of protective bubble of peace. I knew, five weeks after the accident, when my grandma answered the phone at half past six in the morning, Mom was gone. I ran to my room, a strangled scream in my throat, fell to the floor and prayed without words. Gradually a numbing kind of stillness came over me, a sensation of being held.

***

Never one to swear much, I find a torrent of obscenities scream through my mind and sense that something akin to the alien is growing in my chest. Fear makes us restless and TV isn't able to distract. In the evening, Howard and I set out in the dark for our regular walk. We skirt round the subject that monopolises our minds and talk about everyday things, details.

'Did you pay the milk man?'

'I have to go to Stratford on Monday.'

'David needs some more trousers.'

It's lonely and I've never felt like this with Howard. I'm blind to the scattering of lights shimmering in the valley below us and the moon silvering the edges of the clouds above. I shiver in the darkness, although it isn't cold.

Gradually, the exercise and the familiarity of the closeness loosen the stranglehold enough for me to grip hold of every scrap of courage I possess. I whisper the question that is torturing me. 'We're not going to lose him, are we?'

There is silence and I hold my breath. I can imagine the clenched muscles of Howard's face.

'We might,' is his choked reply.

It's not the answer I want, and I gasp as it slices through me, but it's honest. Somehow, voicing that dreadful fear, forces the monster filling my chest into the open where we can share the burden of it.

*

Trust is essential. When I was growing up, casual sex was common in my high school. But it wasn't something I aspired to. I'd seen the devastation experienced by my friends when immature boys treated their 'gifts' with disdain. I wanted something better for myself. My older, long-term boyfriend was not enamoured by this but went along with it. When he went off to university, I suffered the drama of a long-distance relationship.

He only lasted a term away then came back home. But within a few weeks he stopped phoning or calling round.

Eventually, I phoned him. I felt like I was handling an unexploded bomb and tried to keep my tone as light as possible. 'Hi Bill. It's me.'

'Uh… hi.' His reply was stiff, guarded.

'Is everything OK? Only I haven't seen or heard from you for ages.' My stomach was twisting painfully but I was determined to escape the limbo of uncertainty I'd been living in.

'You wouldn't understand,' he said.

Now sweaty anger stamped on my quivering heart and gave me the grit to voice the fear I didn't want to admit.

'Let's see if this is what you mean. There is someone else and you don't want to see me anymore. Is that about right?'

'Yeah,' he said in a small voice.

The blazing strength had nearly dissipated and I was only able to manage a feeble slamming down of the phone. I was heartbroken. I couldn't eat, sleep or imagine my life without him. Seeing him with his new pretty blonde girlfriend was like being wrapped in razor wire.

Then suddenly, after a few months, he was back. I felt triumphant, absolved. But it wasn't long before I realised I actually didn't want him anymore. The relationship had changed. I couldn't trust him.

Howard and I began our relationship in complete honesty. We each tried to give the other as full a picture as possible of our past life experiences. This was painful and quite challenging as it brought out jealousies, insecurity and disapproval. I don't know if this was absolutely necessary but, for us, we started as we meant to go on. We had no secrets that could ambush us and I don't think there's anything that we can't discuss.

***

'Have you got everything?'

'Yeees, Mum,' the boys answer in unison, dragging out the word to emphasise their impatience with my fussing.

'Ring if it's too much and I'll come and get you.'

James ignores this and hurries out after his brother, eager to be with his friends and start the new term.

The door bangs shut and a quiet stuffed with worries settles over me. Summer's over and for the first time, since David was four, I'm not going back to school myself. Autopilot switches on and I move through my days cleaning, preparing, making resources for school. I try to stay near in case James should phone. My life is holding its breath, waiting, oddly disconnected.

David and Howard both travel to Germany but not together. Howard is off to the Motor Show for work and David to stay with Hannah, the exchange student we'd hosted the previous school year. He has grown up so much and become so independent that it's ages before he phones to let us know he's OK. He's having an absolutely wonderful time and claims that Hannah is less wild under the watchful eyes of her parents. They are seeing and doing lots of interesting things and he's making new friends, including an older girlfriend...

*

The day that James had come out of hospital following the initial operation, before we knew it was cancer, Hannah arrived at our house. She looked about 18, complete with spiked hair and pierced nose, but was, in fact, 14 years old. When asked what she'd like to do, she said she liked to go to pubs, clubs and discos. To begin with, she managed to lose her handbag and thought all of her money was in it (fortunately it wasn't) so her first sightseeing trip was to the police station.

When Howard went to collect a group of the students from bowling, they were all there having fun, except Hannah who was at the bar with a lager in her hand. When I came home from work on Tuesday, it was to find she'd dyed her hair, and several of my towels, purple.

I went to pick them up from a party and there was no Hannah. Thankfully, I met her and a friend coming up the street frantically trying to hide something from me. I offered the friend a lift home, to save her hosts a trip out, but Hannah pretended not to understand, trying to get me to let her stay later and come home with her friend. Two can play at that game, though, so I pretended not to understand her and told her to get in the car. On her final full day we planned a picnic with another host family and ended up picnicking together, sharing exchange student stories, whilst the two girls went off shopping.

On the positive side, she was a very pleasant, cheerful girl and easier to talk to than the French boy we'd had the previous year for James.

***

It's the third round of chemotherapy and I spend the day by James' bed, as the poison is dripped into his body. We have devised ways to pass the time and keep his spirits up. I wheel him down, via the lift, to browse in the shop and treat him to magazines and snacks. He drags his drip trolley along like a dog. Or I run him an extravagant bubble bath and stand guard outside the bathroom door to protect his privacy (patients are not allowed to lock the door in case of emergency). If he's well enough, I wheel him round to the hospital school room, where he can use the computers to help his revision. If there's a gap between bags of chemo, we escape from 'hospital world' and sneak out to the cinema for a couple of hours.

Howard arrives on his way home from work so I wearily return to my car to go home to David. There isn't anything like enough parking for the hospital so I've had to abandon my car, along with hundreds of others, on waste land nearby. Shards of glass sparkle in the evening sun. Someone has smashed the window behind the driver's seat. I'm parked under a security camera and the car is alarmed so nothing's been stolen. Apparently, it had just been done for fun.

Parking is one of those irritating problems that add an extra bucketful of stress to an already difficult situation and I fervently wish hospital planners would take this basic need into consideration. I drive home sitting on glass with the wind howling in, but at least it isn't raining. David kindly goes with me to the window repair place where they fit a new window and vacuum out the splinters of glass.

*

James' modesty in the face of all the hospital indignities reminds me of when he was preparing to go to high school for the first time. Howard felt it was time to have the 'Father and Son Talk' and arranged for the two of them to spend a day out together. When James realised what his dad had in mind, he panicked, climbed out through the bathroom window and ran up the road in his socks. Spotting him, our good friends, Pat and Dave, phoned up in alarm to find out what had happened. Once reassured, James and his dad had a lovely day and discussed a wide range of topics, which we hoped would help him in the years to come.

James' reaction seems more understandable once the dynamics of his relationship with Howard are appreciated. When James first started attending the discos his friends seemed to favour for their thirteenth birthday parties, Howard dressed up in the most ridiculous clothes possible and offered to take him to the party. James nearly died of horror and I had to take him in the end. His dad, dressed more appropriately, arrived early to collect him and, after much heated negotiation, was allowed to wait inside until the party finished. Howard asserts that he watched James dance with a girl, return her to the line of those waiting and say, "Right, whose next?" James denies this.

One of the boys' favourite games as children was to hide in the pitch darkness of their bedrooms, with their friends, and have their dad come looking for them as the Tickle Monster. Howard would make roaring monster noises and they would squeal with delight. James stopped letting us kiss him goodnight, aged six, when Howard and his cousin teased him about his missing milk teeth being the result of kissing girls.

***

I'm holding back from God, afraid to trust in His will in case it means I will lose James, as I lost my mother. The air is thin, like walking on the sharp, slippery edge of a mountain's spine, nothing but deep, screaming emptiness on either side. Howard is angry and confused that a supposedly loving God can allow this to happen to children and I have no answer to that. My faith is challenged by him and others. But I know that if I let go of God's hand, I will be lost.

By the time of the fourth chemotherapy, I'm in quite a state. James' leg is huge and painful. The toxic chemicals aren't enough to halt the growth of the tumour. We meet up with Agnes and Foluso (the boy with a rare form of kidney cancer) at the clinic. The routine is to see the doctor and have several tests in the morning before being admitted to the hospital to begin the treatment later in the day.

After the initial check ups, Agnes is excited about something and invites us to her nearby home for our lunch. When we last met, I'd told her about the trouble I was having with my prayers.

Agnes sends the boys off to play on the computer and begins to assemble the ingredients for her amazing rice dish. The bright kitchen fills with delicious aromas.

'I've shared your prayer problems with my other Christian friends. They've assured me that we must ask God for what we want. In Matthew 7:9-11 we're told: *Would any of you who are fathers give your son a stone when he asks for bread? Or would you give him a snake when he asks for a fish? Bad as you are, you know how to give good things to your children. How much more, then, will your Father in heaven give good things to those who ask him!'* Agnes' huge grin reflects the relief I feel.

In the evening, Howard's brother, Simeon, phones and I tell him what Agnes said.

'You're not going to believe it,' his voice is excited, 'I'm ringing because I felt compelled to share the parable of the persistent widow with you. It's the story, in Luke chapter 8, about the poor widow who's been cheated. She goes every day to complain to the judge to do something. He's not a good man, or God-fearing but he helps her just to get rid of her. In verse 7, *Now, will God not judge in favour of his own people who cry to him day and night for help? Will he be slow to help them?'*

At last, I feel able to pray for my heart's desire and to hope that my prayers will be answered. I thank God for reaching out to me through these people and His word.

That night and the following day, as I drive to the hospital, I pray and pray for James to get well. When I finish my prayers, I listen to the radio, park the car, pop in to see James then nip to the toilet. As I walk back to the ward, across the star tiled in the centre of the small foyer at the top of the stairs, I distinctly hear a voice in my head say, 'James will be all right.'

Icy prickles flame my skin and I stop. The area around me is empty. I'm alone in the foyer. I know it isn't my voice in my head because I clearly hear myself cry, *'What?'*

The first voice calmly repeats, 'James will be all right'. The knotted fears in my chest burst open and I blush to think that God should speak to *me*.

Good for you James.

I run to tell James but not even his retort, 'What if He means I'll be alright in heaven?' or the mounting physical evidence to the contrary, can steal the nugget of peace or the feeling of sheer wonder fully away.

*

I've had several experiences of that peace of God, the tiny stillness deep in my core where I'm certain of Him. Despite whatever panic, horror or chaos is going on round me, I know I'm loved and will be given whatever I need to face whatever comes. Just as when my mother died, the peace doesn't keep horrible things from happening but it enables me to cope, to learn and to go on. This is the essence of a life less lost. I'm stumbling along just like everyone else but I know I'm not alone and there is a plan for me, even if I don't know what it is.

Another time when God's peace made all the difference had to do with our finances. Howard enjoyed the physical work of tyre fitting, being his own boss and managing youngsters on training schemes. When Brian finally decided to sell the business to a larger company that had a few other tyre fitting outlets, Howard was made a director and got a pay rise, more responsibility and a better car.

Then, like a crack of summer lightening, Howard came home from work early one day to tell me the receivers were in, he was out of a job. His body was tense and there was a catch in his voice with the effort of marshalling his churning emotions. The owner of the company was not all that he'd appeared to be. Howard had not been involved in the financial aspects of the business and, in his inexperience, had no inkling of any problems until the axe fell. Our children were two and four years old. I was taking time off teaching to look after them. We had no income and very little savings.

Because Howard was a 'director', the company car we enjoyed had to be returned but we were left with the repayments. What would it mean? Should Howard have another try at being a teacher? How long would he be unemployed? How would we manage?

Howard punished himself wondering if he'd missed something that could have enabled him to see it coming, to have prevented this disaster. His self-esteem took a blow just when he would need all his confidence to find a new job.

He applied for all kinds of employment. One of the hardest aspects of redundancy is the suddenly uncertain future. Being human, we kid ourselves that we know what tomorrow will bring. Trying to plan and make decisions when you don't know when or if you'll work again, is incredibly stressful.

One company called Howard back for a third interview and our hopes were running very high. When Howard phoned to say the other candidate had been given the position, I could hear the despair in his voice. A wordless 'arrow' prayer was answered in an instant and I felt an unexpected, peaceful calm, an assurance that something better was in store. Somehow I was able to convey that to Howard with absolute conviction.

One of the silver linings in black clouds is often discovering the potency of friendship. My aunt and cousins came to visit during this time and took us out for treats, someone loaned us a car, a friend let Howard work in exchange for petrol and many more people lent a hand. My cousin, Suzanne, a single mother herself, hid money around the house so we would find it later. Christine and Tony invited us for a meal and encouraged us to explain our situation.

At a subsequent business meeting, Tony gave Howard's details to a man called Darrell. He was looking for someone to help set up a small group of tyre and exhaust outlets as part of an expansion of the existing company, a chain of retail shops selling motor accessories. Within a day or two, Howard was in Darrell's office having a 'chat'. The boys and I were waiting at a nearby supermarket and I felt as though my stomach was being whisked as the time crept by.

Howard got the job. It was a position within travelling distance and was ideal, as opposed to the job we'd been hoping for when he'd made it to the third interview. Had he been successful then, he would have had to travel to

Northern Ireland and be away from home three or four nights a week. God's fingerprints were everywhere.

***

The chemotherapy is adjusted, but the tumour continues to grow. James is in constant pain. I can see it in the pinched muscles of his face and the old-man movements of his body. His skin has a sea-sick pallor. He doesn't complain but he is quiet, a sure sign that things are bad.

I don't want to think what this means. The long wait in clinic to see the doctor is even harder than usual. I can't sit still, can't concentrate on reading, can't think of anything to talk to James about. He's ignoring me anyway, trying to vanish into a hand held game. The air is stuffy, laden with smells I don't want to identify. The room is full of people.

A play coordinator tries to engage the younger children. Some of them are swollen with steroids, tubes snaking from their noses; some are stick thin, hairless and unnaturally quiet. But most continue to play, tussle over the best toys or beg for treats. This isn't our normal pre-chemo appointment so the families we've come to know aren't here today. The parents are subdued. We look like naughty children waiting outside a headmaster's office to hear our punishment. We must have done something horribly wrong; we just don't know what it is.

I don't want to hear the words that confirm what I can see with my own eyes. But they slice through me anyway. Dr Edwards has made us an appointment to begin radiotherapy alongside the chemotherapy. There is a sense of desperation in this suggestion, a subtle implication in the way he looks at me that we should begin to prepare ourselves for the worst.

*

When it was David's turn for the 'Father and Son Talk', he was more prepared and endured it with less drama than James. David soon settled into high school and we were relieved to learn that he was doing well because he was often negative in his comments about homework and school in general. He didn't have any time for the 'in-crowd' but seemed to make friends with people who were on the fringe of things. One friend called for him each morning to walk to school and they made a most unusual pair. David was growing at speed and fast approaching the six foot two inches he would finish at. His friend on the other hand was one of the shortest boys in the class and just to complete the picture had the most amazing, long, bushy hair that seemed to grow straight out from the side of his head. David also befriended another boy, Tom, who was new to the school. His parents, Tim and Hazel, joined our 'Badminton Buddies'.

We never worried about David succumbing to peer pressure, as he seemed to have a clear desire for self-preservation and personal comfort. He was perfectly happy to take himself off to bed early if he was tired, wasn't interested in drinking to excess because he didn't like the way it made him feel and I doubt he could be enticed to try drugs or any of the other teen temptations that have risks attached. We worried sometimes at his quietness and fear of performing, yet this care for himself spoke of a deeper, more secure foundation of self-esteem.

James, on the other hand, who came across as extremely confident, thrived on being the centre of attention. He was intensely aware of appearances and what his friends might think. We were fairly certain he would go along with any daft or dangerous suggestion made by a friend, despite what his conscience might tell him. This made his teen years full of difficulty and meant we were often at odds. Fortunately, he was blessed with quite a large circle of exceptional young men as friends, who cared enough to look out for him when they could. But he also had a few friends who were as daft as he was and it was often a volatile combination.

***

The hospital where James will receive radiation treatment is even further away from home than the oncology unit. At the first appointment, we meet the consultant. He barely looks at us, focuses instead on his notes and James' leg, snapping orders at various minions. We're sent away and another appointment is made. More tests are done and there are no discussions.

Another appointment follows. In all it's four weeks of consultations and preparations, which include making a rigid plastic 'mask' designed to hold the body part in exactly the same position for each blast of radiation, before treatment begins. All the while, James' tumour is clearly growing and I'm swamped by fears that it will spread.

The first day of radiotherapy arrives, at last. I collect James from school and we hurry to get to our appointment on time. Just as I pull onto the busy motorway, the steering wheel jerks in my hand and I'm forced to wrestle the car onto the hard shoulder. The rear tyre nearest the traffic has a puncture. With James shouting words of encouragement and cars and lorries buffeting past me at 70+mph, I manage to change the tyre and we're only a few minutes late. It's amazing how *relative* unpleasant things can be and how uplifting it can be to discover what you're capable of when you have to be.

The mask, which was based on measurements taken three weeks earlier, is already too tight for James' leg. He is squeezed into it anyway. Because the calculations are so exact and recorded on the plastic, it isn't possible to start again. They cut away some sections to try to make it more bearable but it's still excruciatingly painful. The radiotherapy also makes his leg swell; the skin is red and sore like sunburn.

It's over an hour's drive each way to the hospital in which James receives this treatment, with waits that vary from 15 minutes to 2 ½ hours. We go five days a week, for nearly three weeks.

There is a woman there who has lost much of her face to cancer but always seems to have a smile and a ready laugh, which inspires me when I'm tempted to sink into any small pit of self-pity. We realise how fortunate we are to have our own car, as many people have to rely on friends or hospital transport, which basically takes all day.

James manages to go to school in the mornings. He needs his friends, normality and the challenge of his GCSE studies to keep him balanced and positive. The teachers are extremely supportive. One offers us the use of her holiday home, if we need a break. Many offer help out of school hours, if

James feels he needs it. His French teacher makes tapes for us to use on the long car journeys, to help him with listening skills and pronunciation.

*

Cars are certainly a mixed blessing. As David approached school age I began to look for a teaching job. I wasn't having any success with my job applications so decided to put my name on the supply (substitute) teacher list and was quite surprised when I was given work immediately. Fortunately, Howard's brothers, Matthew and Simeon and Matthew's girlfriend, Alison, were on holiday from university, staying with us and could look after the boys. My Dad and brother came to visit in January and were also lumbered with babysitting. I was disappointed to be asked to work on David's first day of school but the head teacher was so desperate that he was prepared for me to come late and go early so that I could take and collect David myself.

It very quickly became clear that I couldn't manage without a car. With only one bus per hour to our village and schools phoning in the mornings that were not on or near the bus route, it was impossible to get to work or be back in time for my children. We took the risk and purchased a bright yellow, six year old, Mini Metro. As it turned out, I was asked to work at least one day a week for the two months I remained on supply before I got a part-time teaching job.

Not long after that, we finished the improvements to our home and decided to continue to climb the housing ladder, hopefully to a place with a larger garden for our growing boys. Unfortunately, we found the house we wanted to buy just as my Aunt Joy, Uncle Glen, Dad and his new girlfriend, Lynda, came for a visit from the States. It was only unfortunate because it meant that Howard had to stay at home, to try to sell our house, on their final weekend, when we'd planned to go to the Lake District.

We were delighted that they'd come. We liked Lynda immediately and were relieved to see the changes she'd wrought in my previously stressed-out dad. It was a real treat to show my history-loving auntie so many of the treasures here in England, the starting point for many of the early Americans.

The trip to the Lakes was the first journey of any distance I'd driven on my own. We had a wonderful time together then my visitors went on up to Scotland and I drove home with the boys. It was a bank holiday weekend and the roads were very busy.

The long queue of traffic wound steadily along the twisting country road, when suddenly a lunatic decided to try to overtake us all. Just as he came alongside me, another driver pulled out from a petrol station without looking both ways. In an instant, the first driver swerved in front of me and clipped my bumper, sending it spiralling skyward in an explosion of noise.

Anxious for my children and plagued by memories of my mother, I pulled in, badly shaken. The other driver sped off. However, several considerate people did stop to see if I was OK and to lend assistance.

Collecting my bumper, I drove on to the first café where I stopped to have a drink and try to quieten my jittery nerves. I was sitting, a shivering wreck, pretending to be normal for the boys, when a man came in and seemed to scan the room.

'Are you the woman from the yellow mini?' he asked, his eyes resting on me.

'Yes,' I replied cautiously.

'I saw what happened to you and I chased after the other driver. I flashed him to stop but he wouldn't.' Reaching into his pocket he offered me a slip of paper. 'Here is the licence number of the car that hit you and this is my name and phone number. I suggest you go straight to the police.'

Overwhelmed by this stranger's kindness, all I could do was offer my grateful thanks and wonder at all the people who had tried to help me despite the tiresome drive and their own needs.

Once I'd reported it to the police I phoned Howard, longing for the comfort of his voice. Shortly after my phone call, his mum phoned to tell him she'd inadvertently set her hedge on fire. She'd contacted him, in a panic, before calling the fire brigade. We've teased Howard ever since that he would never be able to cope with 'another woman' as long as he had the two of us to look after.

That old mini gave me several years of trusty service but once it passed its tenth birthday we began to fall out. After replacing the brakes, I was just revelling in the novelty of being able to stop when and where I wished, when the car decided it would prefer to stop at times and places of its choosing, usually in the middle of nowhere. One night in the snow and dark, Howard had to go down a cobbled farm track, thick with cow muck and try to tow me to the garage for repairs.

Worse than the inconvenience, was the anxiety caused by not knowing if I would be on time to pick up my children or get to work. Eventually, as the unexpected and seemingly never-ending cost of keeping my old banger on the road continued to rise, we took the plunge and bought a new car. It was a Fiat Panda with a tiny engine and just the basics and I was thrilled.

Travelling home from work one evening, down a straight country lane, I noticed an elderly man pulling out from an enclosed entrance. He was carefully watching to see that nothing was coming up the hill on his right and I naturally assumed he would at some point check that all was clear on his left. By the time it was obvious he wasn't going to do that and that he would require the whole of the road to pull his Jaguar through the narrow gate, I only had time to slam my brakes on and squeeze as far into the stone wall as possible. It wasn't enough. He smashed into the front wheel arch, which just crumpled like so much tin foil. I dread to think what would have happened if it had been my door instead. The car was a complete write-off but at least no one was hurt.

Howard happened to be in London at the time so, feeling rather shaken, I was reading quietly after tea. Not for long, though. Investigating a kafuffle in the boy's room, I discovered that James had spilt black enamel paint on David's carpet. Then when David had run to fetch some turpentine to clean it, he'd found his hamster had died.

James' hamster had passed away a few weeks previously and then seemed to come back to life briefly when we massaged him by the fire, only to die again once and for all. These experiences gave him nightmares and engendered a lot of discussion about our mortality.

Not long after this, we received a copy of a letter sent to our insurance company's solicitor from the man who'd smashed into my car. It explained how the accident was entirely my fault, as I had been thinking about what to fix my children for tea rather than concentrating on my driving. Howard wisely suggested I go write my own version of events in a letter of response. Having well and truly vented my spleen, he read the letter then suggested I go write one we could actually send. Ultimately, the other driver had to accept full responsibility and his insurance replaced my car.

***

With the fourth chemotherapy behind us, James has to have all the full body tests again in what they call 'restaging'. We go back to the horrible heart hospital, then to two other Leeds hospitals for a CT scan, a bone scan, kidney tests and a general anaesthetic for two bone marrow tests. James has to drink a litre of radioactive contrasts for the CT, which tastes disgusting he says, and scares me senseless. We are in three hospitals in one day.

It's Howard's fortieth birthday and we manage to have a mini-surprise party for him, with help from his Mum and sister, Louise, who make most of the food. His cousin, Michael, drives all the way down from Scotland to be part of the surprise. James puts a brave face on and joins in with the party games and we all have a good time. I can't help but remember the brilliant treat I had on my fortieth and feel heartbroken that my lovely husband has only this subdued celebration by comparison. The following night he has a drink with his workmates at a local pub, then takes the next five days off (for a mini-holiday, not a hangover).

On Friday, we collect the boys from school, stop off for the radiotherapy treatment and then drive on to a village called Stone in Staffordshire. We have collected vouchers to stay at a Country Club Hotel with satellite TV in the rooms, a pool and mini-gym. David and I splash about in the pool and play on the exercise machines. Howard enjoys not having to rush anywhere or answer phones.

James is pale and listless. It's clear that he feels dreadful but still manages a swim and watches a few films on TV.

We eat in nice restaurants and choose delicious sounding meals but I'm unable to taste my food, as James pushes his around the plate. On Saturday, we visit Jodrell Bank observatory. There's a planetarium, museum with hands-on exhibits and an outdoor environmental centre with paths accessible for wheelchairs, enough to distract James and spark his interest so we all enjoy the day. We can't agree on what to do on Sunday so just end up driving ·the scenic route home through the beautiful Peak District. A soft rain blurs the countryside and seems to blanket our chatter. We stop and order giant sandwiches, which we can't finish.

The following weekend, our wonderful friends and neighbours, Pat and Dave, take James and David to the cinema, keep them for a sleepover and then on to Alton Towers theme park in the morning. They have a fantastic time and are full of stories about the various rides and how they were able to queue jump once or twice because of the wheel chair. It helps James to have something positive made out of the thing that usually inspires pity.

It's good for James and me to have a break from one another. Howard and I have a lovely meal out together. We're all able to restore a bit of strength ready for what is to come next.

*

When the boys were five and seven years old we moved to a house with a bigger garden and a strip of woodland running behind, perfect for rope swings and dens. We'd tripled the value of our previous property and planned to build an extension on this thirty-year-old, two-bedroom, split-level bungalow.

Within eight months of moving, Howard was invited to be part of a management buyout at work. This meant we would be shareholders in the company, for better or worse. It also meant we had to invest every bit of the money we'd put to one side for our extension, plus borrow a bit more. It was a risk, but we both felt it was a calculated risk, because Howard would be part of the team making the company work. It had that 'right' feel, as when it's something God wants you to do.

Being part of a team, making decisions and sharing responsibility for the success of the company gave Howard new interest, enthusiasm and drive. As the company's purchasing director, he also enjoyed trips to various motor shows across Europe and social events including theatre trips, meals, clay pigeon shooting and opportunities to drive in racing cars or watch rally driving. Sometimes I was invited but more often than not he was to go on his own. Yet as busy as he was, caught up in this high-powered, more glamorous life, I knew his family was still central to him. He told funny stories about the things he'd seen in the red light districts of various European cities and the 'most macho' competitions, like who can stay up the latest and drink the most, that business men have when they're away from home.

The children had mixed feelings about the move. James, having just turned seven and with two front teeth missing, started sucking his thumb. When I asked him if he didn't think he was a little old for that, he told me he knew someone on 'the edge of thirteen' that sucked their thumb, so what could I say?

David had only 2½ terms of school experience and wasn't yet a fluent reader. The new school had a different reading scheme and he suddenly lost all confidence. He also began to scream and fight against going to school, which was very distressing for us both. Thankfully, as a teacher, I was able to bring word games home and restore his pleasure in reading, which helped a bit but he never really enjoyed school again. He did seem happier the following year and when I mentioned it to another parent, she told me that his previous teacher didn't like boys.

It was an old-fashioned school in a modern building. Boys had to wear shorts all year round and parents weren't allowed past the school gates. We had to stand in a long line, peering over the hedge, until the teachers came out and collected the children for the day. It was a nice way to meet the other mothers, though. One mum invited me to a party in her home and it turned out she knew Howard from their school days.

Parents weren't allowed to help in classrooms either but I was determined to find a way to ease David's unhappiness. I eventually managed to get past the high security by volunteering to help teach computer skills to the children and was given a cupboard to work in.

A boy, Jim, from James' swimming lessons lived one house up from ours. His birthday came between James' and David's and they all shared a passion for films and the outdoors. The two families developed lasting friendships. Jim's two-year-old sister, Lucy, tickled us all by declaring that blonde Howard reminded her of Desmond Tutu. We think it had something to do with the smiles.

Jim's mum, Pat, is even taller than me, stunning, thoughtful and very sociable. She has a flair for organising outings and parties. His dad, Dave, used to play football in his youth, has a deep, mumbley sort of voice and a wicked sense of humour. Pat and Dave soon joined our weekly badminton games along with good friends of theirs, Ed and Lyn.

When we first moved in, I contacted the school to see if they could put me in touch with someone who would have my children for about quarter of an hour and take them to school on the mornings that I had to be at work. We made an arrangement with a kind neighbour that had a son David's age. Unfortunately, the boys didn't really hit it off. By the time David had a plastic spade thrown at him, resulting in stitches in his head, and James had received a black eye, we agreed I needed to find an alternative solution. The local child-minder charged an extortionate rate and had a manner that I couldn't warm to. Thankfully, Pat stepped in and offered her support.

Chapter 3

I call heaven and earth to witness against you this day, that I have set before you life and death, blessing and curse; therefore choose life, that you and your descendants may live, Deuteronomy 30:19

James is due to have his fifth round of chemotherapy and we wait to be given the results of the re-staging tests. Howard has taken the morning off to be with us. I feel sick, my icy skin sweats. I can smell fear's sour stink. We want a miracle. James' leg has continued to swell, he is drawing into himself. Pain and poisons rob him of his appetite and sparkle. He is bone thin; his eyes are dark and flat, skin waxy.

The news is mixed. There is still no sign of cancer anywhere else. We cling to this morsel. Months of learning have taught us that metastasized cancers are more difficult to treat.

The devastating news, that we have tried to block from our minds but is clear to see, is that neither the radiotherapy nor chemotherapy is stopping the growth of the tumour. In order to save his life, James will have to have an above-the-knee amputation, as soon as possible.

Because of his age, James must give his consent. He cannot be forced to have the operation, even if it means he will die without it. We are to return to see Dr Edwards on Monday, in case the swelling is oedema from the radiotherapy but we suspect this is really only a tiny buffer of hope to ease the shock for James.

We're sent to see another consultant, at a different hospital, about artificial limbs. She is very detached and officious. Her sentences are hard and clipped.

'We will fit you for your prosthesis within a week of your surgery.'

'It takes several weeks to make it up once the measurements are taken.'

'It's more difficult to learn to walk with an above-the-knee amputation.'

No, you won't be able to run or do the things you can do now.'

On and on she goes, nailing pessimistic words and phrases into us. I hate this woman, this stranger. I'm terrified she'll persuade James to give up, to refuse to have the operation. I can't stand it any longer.

'Why are you being so negative? People manage with artificial limbs. He will be able to walk, to lead a normal life.'

'I don't want James to think it will be easy and he'll be up and running straight away. That will only make him frustrated and depressed.'

And this is supposed to spare him from depression? I wonder. I want to tell her that she will have to have an amputation tomorrow and see if she wants every scrap of hope and optimism snatched from under her. But I haven't the strength. A swamp of cold dark fear is closing over me.

We meet a youngish physiotherapist, as we stagger from the consultant's office. He is cheerful and bouncy, exactly what we need.

'How old are you, James,' he asks.

'Fifteen.'

'Well the good news is you'll probably be eligible for a mobility allowance and the DVLA will allow you to begin to learn to drive a year earlier, at 16.'

I want to hug this man and clutch at this information like a buoyancy aid.

James won't talk about any of it on the way home. Gradually, over the weekend we see glimpses of what his thoughts are. He's convinced there must be some other way and that his dad and I are behind this rush to take his leg off. He spits angry words at us, blaming us for not trying hard enough to find an alternative. He believes he will never be able to lead a normal life, get married or have a good job. He draws pictures of one-legged people and leaves them lying around the house.

His friends are marvellous. Where I would have expected teenagers to avoid anything this scary and unknown; they visit, phone, bring cards, gifts and words of encouragement.

I manage to make an appointment for James and David to see a psychologist on Monday afternoon but when I tell David, he runs away. Eventually, he comes back and reluctantly spends about 15 minutes with Mr English. Afterwards, he talks to me more than he's ever done before and I try to reassure him about how important he is to James and how very proud we are of him.

*

The teenage years are difficult for everyone. The transition from child to adult is seldom a smooth glide, as we try to discover who we are as individuals and where we fit with our peers and in the community. It's probably not the easiest time to have a seriously-ill brother or lose a leg or a mother.

Just as I'd once talked with my mother in the seclusion of my bedroom, I began to share my thoughts and fears with God, after her death. As a child, unburdened by concerns over how to pray 'properly', I just told Him everything, thanked Him for the simple blessings I'd begun to appreciate and asked Him for help with my problems. Despite the comfort this brought me, grief would still overwhelm me at times.

Anxious for my dad, I tried to manage my feelings and help him as much as possible. I found I was beginning to know my earthly father in new ways too. He began to talk to me about ordinary domestic things.

One evening, when I was studying in my bedroom, Dad came in with a white envelope in his hand. Somehow he looked like a beaten old man and a trembling little boy at the same time. Never one to discuss his innermost thoughts or feelings, I could see he needed something from me but I didn't know what it was. Thoughts fluttered against the walls of my mind, tiny frightened birds flown in through a window and unable to find the way out, trapped.

He tried to speak, 'Your mom… I…' Then he set the envelope down on my dresser and went out.

It was a birthday card, flowery and sentimental, proclaiming love always. I hadn't realised it was her birthday. Mom reminded me of these things. I was forced to take another faltering lurch towards growing up and learned to mark the special days of others.

As 'big sister' I tried to comfort my brothers. Keith, at twelve years old, seemed to have turned to stone; he didn't shed a tear at the funeral and didn't want to talk about it. Always a quiet, self-contained child, he withdrew further. Charlie, only eight, just seemed bewildered.

As was fairly typical at the time, my parents had only insured my dad's life yet were committed to the new house and business on the strength of their joint salaries. With my grandmothers taking it in turn to help out, three traumatised children and serious financial difficulties, my dad repressed his own grief and struggled on.

He was not the sort of person who could live comfortably without a companion. At 37, tall, with dark wavy hair and deep blue eyes, he was as sociable as my mom had been. After a while, in desperation, he began dating. This was not something my brothers or I found easy. Being a very private person and of a generation that believed that 'children should be seen and not heard', he didn't discuss the situation with us.

On one particular day, Dad had been called away for a short while and his date was left out of sight, at home. The quarrels between my brother and I were seldom physical but for reasons that are lost in the quirks of time, I found myself sitting on top of Keith holding his hair to the floor.

'I'm going to kill you,' he growled menacingly.

Realising I couldn't sit there all day; I rolled off him and curled up into a ball.

Leaping to his feet, Keith grabbed my hair and kicked me full in the face then ran off, appalled at what he'd done.

With an anguished scream, I ran howling to the bathroom with blood streaming through fingers held round my nose. Rushing through the door I came face to face with the terrified woman cowering in the corner, clutching a towel in front of her like some sort of shield.

Unsurprisingly, we never saw her again.

Despite our unconscious attempts at sabotage, fifteen months after my mother's death, my dad remarried. Nicki was eleven years older than me and eleven years younger than my dad. It didn't help our relationship when I learned of the impending marriage from her seven year old daughter. It can't have been easy for Nicki starting a marriage with four children and lots of baggage.

I already did the housework in exchange for the horse I rented and Nicki frequently added the responsibility for the children's dinner. As newlyweds, she would often take my dad back to their room to share their evening meal privately. I felt I was losing the father I was just getting to know. Instead of the appreciation I had always received from my mother and grandmothers for chores well done, there was either indifference or criticism. In my more melodramatic moments I imagined myself as some sort of Cinderella figure.

The hardest part, though, was the unpredictability and mood swings brought on by drink. Alcohol had never figured highly in our home, my mother had an allergy to it, but Nicki liked a drink. Seldom overtly drunk, it would transform her intelligent insecurity into cruel sarcasm. I felt she was an alcoholic because she drank all day, from a morning orange juice and vodka to a late nightcap, but this wasn't generally recognised for another fifteen years.

One helpful thing Nicki did for me was to take me to a specialist about my tonsils. I'd frequently suffered from 'strep' throat, tonsillitis and other throat ailments. The worst time was when I had to miss a Christmas concert for which I had been rehearsing a solo part for months. Nicki was concerned that I would continue to suffer whilst away from home and it might interfere with my studies when I went to university.

The specialist used a giant Q-tip or cotton bud, dipped it in what he said was a type of acid and touched it to various spots on my tonsils. It didn't hurt at all, apart from the urge to gag, and I was told that it would create scar tissue reducing the possibility of infections. It was certainly a less traumatic treatment than a tonsillectomy. In fact, it has proved to be very effective and I can only remember a few throat infections in the past 40 years.

She also took me to another specialist. For years I had suffered severe cramp as part of my monthly cycle. The black moods, irritability and fatigue seemed to be getting worse and lasting longer. The doctor did a full examination and concluded that I was anaemic. But when we were alone, Nicki challenged me to admit that I was no longer a virgin. She told me the doctor had confirmed it. I felt frightened and betrayed. For a start, it wasn't true unless there was something in the facts of life that I didn't know or understand. Could a doctor discuss things like this with my *stepmother* without telling me? What would my dad think? How could I prove my innocence? All remained unanswered.

In fairness, Nicki did try to make us work as a family. She generously included our relatives from my mom's side, in celebrations and encouraged us to keep in touch. There were many kindnesses and thoughtful deeds. And I did want my dad to be happy and understood that I would, hopefully, be off to university and my own life in a few years. My brothers seemed to get on with her so I determined to make the best of it.

***

On Monday, as suspected, the buffer is removed. The swelling is not oedema. Dr Edwards tells us a bed is booked for James in Birmingham. The surgery will be on Wednesday morning, a week before James' sixteenth birthday.

David is on his half-term holiday so he's able to come with us and stay until Sunday. Howard has to work and will meet us there in the evening. It's a long journey. I feel like I'm driving to an execution. We stop off at Meadowhall on the way and watch the film, Dragonheart, for a shot of escapism. I hope it will give us something else to think and talk about.

The cancer is pouring poisons into James' system now. His temperature keeps spiking and crashing. He's in pain, tired all the time and barely eating. His skin's a jaundiced shade of grey. He's pinched and inward looking. He sleeps most of the way. David takes refuge in his Gameboy and I try to concentrate on driving through my tears.

As soon as we arrive at the hospital, they rush James down to X-ray, as it's nearly 5pm. They've given him a large private room, which we're grateful for, as we'd found the big, open, noisy wards very wearing the last time we'd been in this place. There are two beds in James' room and David thoughtfully offers to stay over night, in case his brother needs him. Howard and I feel guilty sloping off to a hotel and offer to take turns but James prefers his brother's company.

The surgeon comes to visit James in the evening and is superb. A quietly spoken man, he seems young, perhaps in his thirties. He stays for ages patiently answering all of James' questions, thoughtfully and thoroughly. The surgeon promises an extra MRI scan first thing in the morning so that he can clearly show James that this is the only way we can save his life. It's a gift for which I will always be indebted.

He's as good as his word and shows us the results when we get to the theatre at noon the next day. The cancer has grown from the size of a cherry in May to a 25cm long monster that fills the whole of his lower leg. James, groggy from the pre-med, finally gives the surgeon permission to go ahead, as long as he does the best job he can. I kiss him as he drifts off to sleep and remind him not to be sick when he wakes up (power of suggestion).

We wait back on the ward. A junior doctor has told us the operation will take about half an hour so we're pretty worked up an hour and a half later, when a nurse comes to tell us the doctor wants to speak to us on the phone.

'Sorry about the delay,' he says, 'the previous case held things up. The operation has gone very well, with little bleeding and apparently clean, clear tissue.'

The release turns my bones to soggy pasta. I have to remind myself to breath. All those drawings James left lying around the house shocked me and I'm frightened of how I'll respond when I see my mutilated son. Sensations like static electric pin pricks flash round my body. I pray. Somehow my spaghetti legs take me down to the high dependency unit, where we find James awake.

All the previous terror, anxiety and anticipation evaporate and calm relief floods over me. The first thing James asks is for us to look at his stump. He scrutinises our faces to test our reactions. I'm surprised to discover how easy it is. The bandaged limb is neat and part of him; the horrible, scarred, cancer-filled lower leg, gone forever.

James seems satisfied with our responses and drifts in and out of sleep. About 6pm we decide to slip out for something to eat. We walk back into the unit, almost giddy now the tension of the day is behind us. In an instant we're plunged back into fear. James is writhing in agony and the nurse is frantic. They can't control his pain and his blood pressure keeps causing the monitor to cry out in alarm.

The nurse feels the problem is due to a full bladder, which because of the epidural James is unable to relieve, but she isn't allowed to catheterise him herself. For forty minutes she's been trying to get hold of a doctor.

Nothing can describe how it feels to be helpless whilst your child screams in pain and machines tell you he's in danger. Howard and David set off to find a doctor themselves, enlisting the help of the nurses on the ward and finally head for the canteen to drag one from their dinner. Fortunately, a doctor is located before that's necessary.

When she arrives, the doctor walks straight past me, ignoring my frantic gestures and comments that 'he's here, he's here'. At the far end of the unit, I hear the nurse apologise and say, 'I'm sorry, I didn't mean to be rude but we have a patient in pain and very distressed parents'. When I hear the nurse apologise a second time, I have to leave the room. I have never been so close to physically and verbally abusing anyone before in my life and that won't help my son.

David and I go back upstairs to calm down and let the doctor do her work. James asks his dad to wait outside the curtain. He can hear the doctor say, 'I'll need this or that item' and the nurse's restrained reply that everything is ready (and has been for some time).

'Well, I'll need some number 7 gloves.'

'I'm afraid we only have number 8's.'

'Oh, I suppose they'll have to do,' is the snotty reply. 'Right let's have a look here. Wow, look at the size of this!'

Howard nearly chokes before he realises she's talking about the glove. Six hundred and fifty ml of urine lighter and James' pain subsides. Needless to say, I spend the night with James and the following day they take him back to his room on the main ward.

*

That's not to say I never lose my temper. Our second house was an end-terrace and had a shared yard with an entrance directly into the road, nearest my house. There was also access up steps, in two places, along the lane running behind. The gate at my end was broken so, when I let the dog out and the children were playing, I would wedge an old door against the opening, held in place by the dustbin.

One day, as three-year-old David and a little friend played just outside the door, I was keeping an ear on them whilst I washed up in the kitchen.

An almighty crash sent the dish slithering through my wet hands and my arms plunged to the elbow in the suds to steady myself.

Nancy, a friend of my neighbour, Mrs Wells, was on her way to visit and barged through my makeshift barrier. Without pausing to lift the old door back into place, this woman stomped past the two shocked children and the now barking dog and left them vulnerable to the road.

Psychedelic green and orange rage exploded in my guts. Securing the door-gate I roared, like a lioness protecting her cubs, down the yard to make my feelings known to this woman.

'Do you realise those children could have been hurt because you left that gate open?' I demanded.

'Your dog bit me,' she said, lifting a clean, unblemished white cardigan to reveal an unharmed arm. 'I'm thinking of reporting it and having your dog put down.'

Anger now clawed its way past any shred of manners I might have possessed. 'If you ever come through my yard like that again, *I'll* bite you,' I growled.

'You must never behave like that in my home towards my visitors again,'

Mrs Wells informed me in a steely voice, as I turned to leave.

For two days my fury steamed through me. I imagined all the things that might have happened, I raged at the woman's ignorance at not using any of the three alternative entrances and more.

At the same time, a different voice in my mind was quietly repeating, *'forgive my trespasses as I forgive those who trespass against me.'* With great persistence, it was made clear that I had to choose. If I wanted my sins, faults and mistakes forgiven then I must forgive this woman. It had to be God's way or the way of the world. I knew I wanted God's way but it wasn't easy. Prayer made it possible.

Gradually, as my own outrage subsided, I remembered the kindness with which Mrs Wells had always treated me. I thought about the charity of the woman who was giving her time to visit this elderly housebound friend of mine. I realised it was our own laziness that resulted in not having a proper, safe gate in place.

Finally, I was able to forgive the woman and went, at the first opportunity, to apologise. It was pretty clear that she had not forgiven me but that did not detract from the restored peace I enjoyed with God.

***

The rest of the week plods on to the beat of hospital time. Howard and I cling to one another in the dark of our hotel room and feel guilty for being whole and finding comfort. A woolly numbness shrouds me and I observe events as though detached.

Howard's brother, Matthew, comes to visit on Friday and stays with James while we go into Birmingham in search of birthday presents. Then in the afternoon, James' friends, Rory and Martin, come to see him, thanks to Rory's mum, Joan, who drives 120 miles each way. On Saturday, Jim and his family, Alex, his parents and friend Sam also make the long journey. On Sunday, Howard's cousin Michael drives for five hours from Scotland to visit. James receives over 70 cards and loads of phone calls, which really cheer him up. He even gets a card from a lady we'd met having radiotherapy and another from the woman who supervised his piano exams. These acts of love and kindness penetrate my emptiness and fill me with wonder.

The doctors keep James on an epidural for three or four days but start him on physiotherapy on the second day after the operation. By Monday, he's able to go down to the gym twice and work out for a total of two and a half hours. He even does another half hour on Tuesday morning before we set off for home.

It's his birthday and the nurses give him a little surprise party before we leave. There's a cake, treats, cards and even a ten-pound gift voucher. The surgeon comes to see James and tells him he's pleased with his progress. He also explains that James' tumour is so rare and unusual that it will be written up in the medical journals.

At last, eager to be on our way, I realise that James is hesitating. He feels I'm rushing him. I imagine he's afraid to be away from medical help and out in the real world where he will have to face other people's reactions and life without his leg.

*

After James was born, I couldn't wait to get home. I shared my hospital room with three other new mothers, one of which had just delivered her sixth son, the other five had all been put in care. She was about my age and was apparently hoping for a girl. Smoking was allowed in the dining room and the food was highly refined. Constipation is not advisable when you've just given birth. As this was my first baby and he was a little jaundiced, I had to stay in for three long days.

When I finally did get home, though, it was really scary. It hit us suddenly how little we knew about looking after a baby and the responsibility for his health and safety seemed enormous. It had been so easy in hospital to feed and bathe James but completely daunting without a trained nurse standing by in case of emergency or just to offer a little advice.

In our small cottage, the nursery had been decorated and curtains made. We'd received many splendid baby gifts, which I frequently admired and showed off in the months before the birth. Howard had refurbished an old cot from his parent's attic and turned a woodworking project from high school into a wardrobe. We'd also purchased some second hand baby equipment from a woman in the village, including a wonderful old-fashioned Silver Cross pram. The woman had been expecting her first grandchild and assumed she was in the 'change' when, instead, she discovered she was pregnant herself. She'd ·bought lovely new things for this unforeseen child and had no intention of having any more children, now that he'd outgrown them.

But we'd still been caught somewhat unprepared for this early arrival and Howard worked his socks off to get everything ready for our homecoming, from ensuring the whole house was toasty warm to the embarrassing purchase of necessary feminine sanitary wear.

We were also worried about the reaction of our Great Dane, Lady, fearing we would have to find her a new home if she showed even the slightest signs of jealousy. But it was obvious from the beginning that Lady regarded this new baby as her own pup and would protect James from any harm.

This was made abundantly clear when the health visitor came to check the baby for click hip. I had run upstairs for a clean nappy whilst she rotated James' legs, making him cry. When I returned, the dog had pinned this amazingly composed woman to the wall with a paw on each shoulder. Lady wasn't growling, barking or hurting her at all, just preventing her from touching the baby.

***

James begins to experience strange pains and on the journey home they become worse. 'Phantom' pains are sensations in the brain from the part of the body that is no longer there so you can't give it a rub or scratch and they are very difficult to relieve. I don't know what to say or do for him and promise to phone the doctor when we get home.

But there isn't time. All of his friends come round in the evening for a mini-birthday party and the fun and laughter is just what we need. One lad gives James a plastic, hairy chest, complete with muscles, for him to prove to the physiotherapist that all the exercises are working. Another brings a card with a press-out garden toupee, which you tie on your head, and magnetic earrings. His friend, Rory, has written him this poem:

> To you our hearts go in sorrow,
> But please try to think of tomorrow
> When Cancer is done
> We can all have some fun
> In your new car that we can borrow.

> I now change from humour and jest
> 'Cos I'm tired and my mind needs a rest
> All I want to say
> On this special day
> Is that Slappy, my friend, you're the best.

> My rhymes must now bite the cud
> So Happy 16th little Bud
> You've been more of a man
> Than most men can
> But your head looks like a peeled spud

*

Like James, friends also became important to me after my mother died. The sympathy people felt for my family encouraged my peers to include me more and, as they got to know me, they liked me. Gradually I overcame the earlier stigma. My best friend, Janie, shared her family with me and I spent as much time as possible at their house. They even took me on vacation with them once, to a big horse show in Tennessee, in their huge Winnebago. Janie had a Tennessee Walking-horse and rode it in the competitions. We also shared a deep self-consciousness about our bodies, their normal imperfections exaggerated in our teenaged imaginations. When we would get home after the hot, dirty work in the barn with our horses, we would jump in the lake and swim to the island in our long blue jeans and tee shirts.

We both enjoyed skiing and were on the school racing team. We had a laugh during training and even relished the pre-season workouts when we had to run up and down stairs, 'sit' against a wall without a chair and other exercises designed to develop our stamina and leg muscles. Belonging in the team put stabilizers back on my wobbly life.

In slalom racing, you ski down the course twice and your times are added together. In one important race, Jane and I actually tied to a hundredth of a second. My dad and Nicki came to watch me ski once or twice but, when I discovered they were there, I was so nervous I fell.

Janie's mom, whom I always respectfully referred to as Mrs Steinhilber, was wonderful to me. She'd married young but was still very much in love with her quiet, somewhat reclusive, husband. Her five children were everything to her and they generously opened their hearts to me and helped me to survive the years before I left home.

When I was upset about my Dad's impending marriage, Mrs Stenhilber made it easier by telling me that he wouldn't have rushed to remarry if he hadn't been so happy the first time round. I spent hours, with Jane, her mom and two sisters, talking round their huge kitchen table, sewing or making cookies.

Thankfully, I found schoolwork easy and the other mothers made it possible for me to be on the ski team by driving me to the events. I had my horse but I also had all the extra work to keep her. I was expected to buy my own clothes so Mrs Steinhilber helped me to make them.

My dad seemed a strict, hard father compared to other parents. He expected us to pay our own way, believing that we would value more the things we'd worked for than those that had been given. He also taught us that he meant what he said, to be responsible for our decisions and accept any consequences of our actions. As a parent myself, I now appreciate that it's harder to do that than to protect your child at all costs, which is a more instinctive response.

Between my heavenly and earthly 'Fathers', I was given the freedom and responsibility to understand that the choices in my life were mine to make and the courage and self-confidence to make them. This didn't stop me from making mistakes but enabled me to try to learn from them.

I was forbidden to attend unchaperoned parties, something unheard of amongst my peers, and the only kind of party they would attend. One evening I was waiting eagerly for Ryan to arrive. He was the popular rebel at school, wearing scruffy clothes and dabbling in drugs. All my friends were envious when they heard he'd asked me out.

'I want to meet this young man before you go,' ordered my dad.

Nervously, I took Ryan into the living room and we sat on the edge of the settee. I couldn't bring myself to look at either of them, hoping perhaps if I couldn't see what was happening then maybe it wouldn't be real.

'What are you studying at school, Ryan?'

'What grades do you get?'

'What are your plans for the future?'

'Do you have a part time job?'

The questions seemed endless. Burning shame battled with blazing fury, my sweaty hands unable to stop trembling. I almost expected Ryan to be asked what toothpaste he used.

Suddenly, my dad stood up. 'I must ask you to leave now. I will not permit you to take my daughter out,' he said, waiting to see Ryan to the door.

Without a word, Ryan went.

'Dad! How could you? Why?' I screamed.

'He's not the sort of person I want you to go out with,' was all he would say, walking away.

'But it's not fair,' I wailed, following. 'Why don't you trust me?'

'I do trust you, it's everyone else I don't trust,' he said.

'You're forcing me to go behind your back,' I challenged.

'You'll have to do what you think is right but you know what my feelings are,' he replied evenly.

Maddeningly, it didn't take me long to decide Ryan wasn't right for me after a few clandestine meetings. I wondered if my dad had a tip off about Ryan because nothing like that happened before or after that incident.

Eventually, fuelled by my sense of injustice, I snuck out to a party. Goaded by my stepmother, phone calls were made and I was discovered. Inexperienced as I was in subterfuge and drinking, my befuddled mind didn't pick up on the clues that I was in big trouble. When asked by my father ·where I'd been, I lied. For the first and only time in my life, my dad hit me, several times in fact, watched and encouraged by Nicki. I was left in no doubt as to the seriousness with which my father regarded lying and I have never overtly lied to him since.

I did, however, attend another unchaperoned party and learned something else the hard way. My friends and I persuaded our parents to let us camp out in a local park. I set to and erected the tents whilst my friends mixed drinks to get us in the party mood. It was a very warm evening and I worked up quite a thirst, downing the alcoholic drinks like the pop that was in them. Before we were ready to leave for the party I was nearly too drunk to stand and have only fleeting, fuzzy memories of the night.

Getting up for my Saturday job in the chemist's shop the next day, I felt worse than I'd ever felt before in my life. Rushing to the basement toilet several times throughout the morning was not an experience I ever hope to repeat. I'm appalled when I think what might have happened to me that night and have never drunk to that level of excess again.

***

The phantom pain is worse. James hides in his room and cries out in despair and frustration. With each new day it intensifies. The doctor tells us that people, who've been in a great deal of pain over a long period of time before an amputation, usually suffer phantom pain the most. It's largely a problem of the mind. The drugs he gives James will take four to six weeks before they begin to reduce the pain, if they work at all. Ordinary painkillers don't help.

The pain is every bit as real as the agony James endured from his poisoned leg but the surgery seems to have knocked the fight out of him. Because there's nothing he can do, like shift position, scratch or rub, the pain is in control. And it's torture for us all.

We return to the hospital to see the oncologist, Dr Edwards. He tells us we have three options.

1.   We can stop treatment now that the leg is gone.
2.   We can finish the course of chemotherapy he's been on. Whilst it hasn't been totally effective on the tumour it would appear that it has kept the cancer from spreading to other parts of his body.
3.   We can start a new course of chemotherapy using different drugs.

We agree on option 2, in case there are any rogue cells still looking for a place to grow. It's the decision recommended by the doctor and the one James prefers. It means he will have three more cycles to take and will be finished by Christmas. It would also give us another set of chemotherapy drugs up our sleeve, if the cancer should reappear, we thought.

Three days after our return from Birmingham, James is back in hospital for his next round of chemotherapy. Unfortunately, this seems to increase the phantom pains. James can't see an end to it, feels he's lost everything and wishes he were dead.

I understand how real this temptation must be. There were times, when I was growing up, that the warmth of Jane's home and family merely heightened the sense of loneliness I felt in my own. One summer's night I lay on the dock that stretched out over the lake, in the dark. I looked into the cold, black water, sprinkled with reflected lights, and wondered about slipping under the surface and out of this life. Somehow I felt stronger for having looked squarely into the heart of this possibility and rejecting it. How much worse must it be for my child? I pray he will resist and find his way back to joy.

We try everything we can think of to distract James from the pain. I continue to take the boys to see the psychologist regularly and he gives us a relaxation tape. I phone the local hospice and they are lovely. Two women come to our house to try aroma- and art therapies. James isn't comfortable about a full aromatherapy massage but allows the therapist to massage his head and neck. I'm offered a treatment, as well, but am so focused on James I can't bring myself to accept. The artist unpacks an array of colours in chalk, crayon, pencil and paint. She gives us paper and leads us into gentle play in our own space. I'm sitting on the carpet in warm sunshine and feel a quiet peace spread through me. James' face is relaxed for the first time in weeks.

*

I am reminded of the problems I had trying to take an art class when I was in high school. Severe overcrowding at my school resulted in an unusual solution. Half the children attended lessons from 7am-12:30 pm and the other half from 1-5:30 pm. The school day was slightly shorter and there was no need for lunch breaks. It meant that pupils with good grades had no choices beyond the college prep classes, which for me meant no time for art. So I opted to take trigonometry at summer school, in order to free up a period during the term to take a jewellery class.

Birddog, a friend whose nickname was inspired from such an obscure source I can't recall it, also went to trigonometry class in summer school and he gave me a lift each day on his big motorbike. He was one of a crowd of friends and because I had often found it easier to relate to boys than girls, I felt very close to him. We had great fun that summer. I was truly distressed when he admitted to having a crush on me and wanting a different kind of relationship. For me it felt almost incestuous to even consider it but I was bereft at losing the closeness of our friendship.

I loved the jewellery class. It was a breath of colour and freedom. My favourite piece was a tiny silver skier that I wore round my neck until I lost it in the lake, swimming. I also made a beaded necklace that I wore to the prom. The art teacher was shocked and, I think, a little disappointed to discover that someone who could do maths could also be creative.

***

Watching my son sink deeper and deeper into misery drags time to a virtual stop. I sizzle inside, desperate to do something. James alternately pleads with me to help him or spits blame.

'I don't know what else to try, Sweetheart.' I feel utterly helpless.

James looks into my face and I see my failure in his eyes. We have betrayed his trust, parents are supposed to protect their children. He walks into his room and shuts the door.

My heart is screaming. I escape to my room, throw myself on the bed and cry out in prayer. 'You promised, Lord, you would never give us burdens too great to carry. I can't bear to see him this way.'

Almost instantly, the phone rings. It's my friend, Pat, asking if I fancy a walk with her. As we walk, I pour out my anguish and she listens. She might not believe it but she's the answer to my prayer, the Spirit is working through her. When I get back, feeling stronger, James also seems to have improved slightly.

He decides he's well enough to go back to school. I can hardly breathe, as I drop him off for his first day with one leg and watch him make his way inside, thin, bald and alone (he insisted on that). The school is very poorly designed for the handicapped. He will have to go up and down several flights of stairs between each class and 'walk' miles of corridors, on crutches, weak from his treatments and major surgery. However, as soon as he faces this challenge, almost imperceptibly, the pains begin to subside. Whether it's the removal of that particular fear from the tempest in his mind or the distraction of lessons and friends, I don't know. Perhaps the drugs have finally kicked in.

Through all of this David is incredible. He quietly copes with his needs taking second place and tries to keep normality for James. He teases his brother brutally, when he senses James becoming morbid or self-pitying, until he gets a laugh or a smile. At school, David has taken on the job of editor of the school paper, helps set up a film club and plays keyboard and saxophone in the orchestra and Big Band. He also has a paper round and is still active in scouts.

Howard is trying to cope with working for the new company. He has to fight his corner and wins a bigger budget for his department and more realistic targets. He earns some long overdue recognition and praise for his hard work and is promised a fairer wage structure and more support. But he's also being asked to work longer and longer hours and be away from home more frequently than ever.

The wonderful surgeon from Birmingham phones me at home, a few weeks after the operation. He tells me that the preliminary pathology reports show 60 to 65% necrosis (dead cancer cells), which means that the chemotherapy was having some effect. The cells had changed since the biopsy in July. The cancer had invaded the small blood vessels and the lymph tissue so there would have been absolutely no way to save the leg. The margins were clear so, hopefully, there would be no more cancer in his body.

*

The power of emotion on physical health wasn't new to me. I was seventeen in the autumn that we loaded up my dad's car to take me the 250 miles to a university on the other side of the state, the one my parents had gone to. There was only one other person I knew from my school who was going to the same university.

I had barely slept, wondering what my new life would be like and, more important, my new roommate. I didn't even know her name. Would I be able to find my way around the campus of a university that had 25,000 students? What would the classes and teachers be like? Would I be able to do the work and find a part time job? As well as the fears, there was the carbonated feeling of excitement; I was getting away, trying new things, beginning to make my own way in the world.

Driving along in the late summer heat, my stomach alternately rolled and clenched. I couldn't seem to deepen my breathing or slow my heart rate.

Into the silence, Nicki casually announced, 'Oh by the way, May will be having your bedroom.'

The image of my ten-year-old stepsister scattering her things carelessly about in my private space, splashed orange and black across my mind. Apart from the fact that, had I known, I could have removed my treasured possessions. I felt like a tiny dinghy cut loose from its moorings at the height of a storm.

'What about when I come home?' I managed to squeeze out of my constricted throat.

'Oh, you won't be coming home,' was the happy reply.

When I recovered the ability to speak, gasping to the surface of my own private tempest, I asked, 'But what about Christmas and Thanksgiving?'

'I guess you could sleep on the couch,' she answered, obviously surprised by the very idea.

My dad made no comment during this 'discussion'. He had perfected the art of 'tuning out' and probably hadn't heard what had been said.

The dorm room was just large enough for its two occupants and we shared a bathroom with the two girls in the next room. I cried most of the first week and can't imagine what my new roommates thought. Managing to beg a lift home the first weekend, my dad opened the door, as I arrived and greeted me with, literally, open arms. That huge hug from my usually undemonstrative father was all that I needed. I didn't shed another tear or return home, except for holidays, until the summer.

I was paying my own way through university, which meant that I had to work part time during the term and full time during the four-month summer break. My Dad and Nicki had sold their house and were living in a small rented place whilst they were having a new home built. Staying with them meant that I could save every penny I earned as a waitress, for the coming year. However, the tension in the house, which I assumed was caused by my presence, and the sarcastic, outwardly inoffensive but hurtful remarks made by Nicki, quickly convinced me that I could never go home again for more than the briefest of visits.

***

James has to continue the physiotherapy he'd begun in Birmingham, to prepare for the artificial leg he is promised in 6 to 8 weeks. He will then need more physiotherapy to help him learn to walk and climb stairs with the prosthesis. There is a rehabilitation unit in the small hospital where we see the psychologist. I pop in to see if I can arrange an appointment for James.

The woman I speak to is kind, softly spoken and about my age.

'Of course, we would be glad to help but I'm not sure if this is the best place for your son,' she explains. 'We specialise in stroke rehabilitation so our patients are mainly elderly. There is a bigger, better-equipped unit, catering for a wider range of patients, at the main hospital in town.'

The grounds of the smaller hospital run alongside the playground of the school where I teach. It would be convenient to be able to bring him here ·once I get back to work. But James' needs come first and I want him to have the best help he can get. We agree that I should take James along to both facilities and let him decide. She makes him an appointment at the other hospital.

The large gymnasium, when we find it through the maze of long, shiny corridors, surprises me. It smells of sweat, floor polish and rubber plimsolls. The ceiling is very high and the wooden floor glows. It reminds me of my high school gym, except it has more and different equipment filling two thirds of the space. Medieval torture chambers come to mind.

A physiotherapist saunters over to us and only partially listens to what I have to say about the phantom pain James is suffering. She sends me to a chair against the wall and bustles James over to a machine. In minutes, she leaves him to get on with it. This alarms me. He is so down at the moment he needs encouragement to keep breathing, never mind work hard on an unfamiliar machine.

I look around the large room. This seems to be the way they normally operate. There is another boy, James' age, with what looks like cerebral palsy, fighting against the straps binding him to a black machine that pumps his arms and legs. A middle-aged man is red faced and damp with the effort of hauling himself between parallel bars. There are elderly people struggling away at various tasks, all looking unsure and miserable. The four therapists, in the meantime, are reading, chatting to each other, arranging flowers and generally oblivious to the patients.

The physiotherapist in Birmingham had been fantastic, helping, encouraging and reassuring James every step of the way. I can't understand how these people can be so different. I'm appalled for all the patients in the room. Prickly outrage is bubbling up.

I look back at James and see that he's in agony and has started across the room towards me. I meet him halfway.

'Are you all right, James?'

'It hurts and I'm not sure how to do it.' He looks down. They've made him feel useless.

'Well don't worry. I am less than impressed with the care you're receiving and we're leaving.' Anger has made my voice loud and it carries with a teacher's authority.

The physiotherapists leap to their feet and rush towards us but we've had enough. I can't bring myself to speak to them. We turn and march from the room. I report my observations to several people in a position to take the matter further but we aren't prepared to go back there.

Happily, the team at the smaller unit are terrific. It's quiet by the time James arrives after school. He has a young physiotherapist all to himself and she's very supportive and positive. There's also another younger boy, eleven years old, who's having help after a below-the-knee amputation. His foot had been crushed in an accident with a bus. This child is very quickly back on his 'feet', not having to contend with chemotherapy or to learn the more complicated skills involved in managing without a knee.

*

Usually, I am a polite, mild-mannered person but injustice brings out the bolshiness in me. As a teenager, I had crushes like everyone else. One day in a geometry class, I was busy composing a love letter, which I wouldn't send, when the teacher called on me to answer a question.

'What is the length of the hypotenuse?'

Glancing up at the board, I gave the correct response and returned to my letter.

Apparently, he'd been hoping to catch me out. Busy as I was, I hadn't detected the scarlet silence that propelled him over to snatch up the letter from under my hand.

Panic stung my mind. *Please don't let anyone read what I've written*, I pleaded silently.

Just then the teacher was called out of the room, dropping my letter onto his desk, as he passed.

Trembling, but furious at the injustice of being punished when I felt I hadn't done anything wrong, I went up and took it back.

Spotting the letter's absence on his return, the teacher screamed at me. 'How dare you take anything off my desk without permission?'

With heart thundering, in a strangled passion, I answered, 'Well, you shouldn't take things off my desk, either.'

This left him with nothing to say in front of the class and fortunately the bell went. I am very grateful that this teacher didn't seem to hold the incident against me.

***

The usual pattern of chemotherapy, once they got the anti-sickness medication right, was for James to be in hospital from Tuesday through Friday whilst the drugs were administered. He then came home but was so weak and nauseous that he stayed in bed until Wednesday.

On the Wednesday after the sixth chemotherapy, James and I are at the prosthetics unit in Leeds. He has one small spot on his scar that still hasn't healed. There is a little scab that keeps coming off when he wears the special silicon stocking that is preparing his stump for the artificial leg. A nurse looks at it and says it's a stitch that hasn't dissolved. She picks up some tweezers and pulls it out.

By Friday it looks worse so we go to our GP. He puts James on strong antibiotics and dresses the area carefully.

Unfortunately, because of the powerful effects of the chemotherapy, James' body just isn't able to fight the infection. He ends up back in hospital for ten days on intravenous antibiotics. That means he only has a few days at home before he has to return for his final chemotherapy. Just enough time to take three 'mock', or practice, GCSE exams, attend the Scout Christmas dinner and receive his chief scout award alongside his brother.

His Uncle Chris drops in for a quick visit, with perfect timing, enabling him to sit with James in hospital whilst Howard and I go to watch David perform in his first concert with the Big Band.

I feel colder inside than the crisp, dark December night against my face. Every action is mechanical. The screamed obscenities have stopped, as if my mind has been quietly shut down by prolonged exposure to hospital time. Howard manages to go with me to the concert. We slide into one of the well-worn wooden pews of the old parish church.

David is tall and easy to see, standing to one side behind the keyboard. There is someone speaking but I am lost in contemplation of my son. A little smile lifts the heavy corner of my mouth and tears prickle at the edge of my eyes. Since their first performances dressed as sheep in their playgroup Nativity plays, I have smiled and wept to see my boys on stage.

The music begins and fills the whole space right up to the soaring ceiling. The familiar sounds of Christmas stroke my senses and thaw my icy core. I try to hold back the tears for David's sake. It's an hour of light and warmth and love, a brief respite.

The next day we are allowed to collect James, between injections, to bring him home so that he can take part in some filming at his school. A television drama, *Where the Heart Is*, is using the building and many of the children are invited to be extras. He gets to appear alongside Sarah Lancashire and Pam Grier. If you look very closely at that episode, you can just make out a bald young man disco dancing on one leg.

*

Howard comes from a family of musical performers. His grandfather had been a choirmaster and his grandmother had taught piano all her life. All six children in his family were singers and even performed on television, in *Stars on Sunday* with Gracie Field. Howard had been short-listed to star in *Oliver* but missed out because he looked too well fed. His sister, Delith, and brother, Matthew, became professional singers as adults, Simeon a music teacher and his sisters, Louise and Lorraine, sing in local groups. Only

Howard, whose voice broke on stage when he was thirteen, gave up singing in public altogether.

Howard's grandma had been looking forward to teaching our children to play piano but she felt they needed to have begun to read first. As soon as David was old enough to pull himself up on the furniture, he tried to climb the piano stool to play. When grandma died, she left her treasured baby grand piano to us and once David was learning to read, we arranged for the boys to have lessons.

As they were early risers, we insisted on ten minutes initially, building to fifteen minutes practise every day before they went to school and were delighted when they chose to play for fun at other times. Because it was a short period of time and part of the routine, in the morning before other distractions might interfere, it worked very well.

They both became quite talented pianists. Howard wanted them to follow in the Brook family footsteps and take part in the local piano competitions. He felt it would give them goals to work toward, self-confidence and a sense of achievement. James, who wanted to take up every opportunity that life offered, wasn't as passionate about music as David and didn't practise as conscientiously as his brother. In the privacy of our home, James' playing was often full of mistakes whilst David's was flawless.

Unfortunately for David, when they got up on the stage something happened. It was as if James had a formal bowtie and tails which he swished out behind, as he sat and responded to the audience with flair and panache; whilst poor David seemed to crumple and stumble under the gaze of others. Howard felt that encouraging him to keep trying would help him to overcome this stage fright, which it did to some extent, but he never liked competitions. At least this problem didn't extend to his piano exams and he received many distinctions for the different grades he took over the years.

David didn't seem to suffer in the same way if there were others on stage with him. When he and James were little they used our wide front lobby as a theatre. Howard and I sat on chairs at the bottom of the five steps while the boys took turns centre stage on the landing above. David sang while James played the piano, they told jokes (have you heard the jokes six-year-olds tell?), did a mime and were generally very silly. My favourite part was when David limped silently, straight faced, with one stiff leg, across the stage behind James as he was telling jokes.

***

James' final chemotherapy comes and goes. I have a 'we've done it!' feeling, as if we've crossed a finishing line. We put a generous cheque into a Christmas card for the cancer ward to thank them for all they've done for our son. Anxious to close a door on the past six months, we look forward and determine to get on with rebuilding our lives. I make arrangements and am very excited to get back to work in the new term, to reclaim my own identity and return to 'normal' life. Mum and Kenneth, Howard's stepfather, offer to help with some of the endless journeys that James will still need to make to various hospitals. I persuade the doctor to have James' full body scans and tests done early so that I can go with him and he won't have to miss any more school than necessary.

There are parties and we throw ourselves into preparations for the holidays. We thoroughly enjoy the high school's Christmas concert, especially since David is accompanying the orchestra on the piano.

There are smiles and tears and millions of photographs as James and his gorgeous date pose before attending their school dinner dance for the final-year students. He looks terrific (if a little pale) in a hired dinner jacket and shiny new waistcoat. He has a fantastic time, even getting up on stage to dance the can-can with his friends.

But a few days before Christmas, James tells me his scar feels funny again. I take him straight to the hospital where they put him back onto IV antibiotics. He is extremely upset and furious with me, as he feels I've over-reacted. However, because we catch it early and his blood responds to the GCSF and the antibiotics, they are able to use a drug that can be injected rather than administered on a drip. James begs them to teach him how to inject it himself into his portacath. Satisfied that he can do it, they let us take him home on Christmas Eve.

But there are many children who are not so fortunate, who spend their 'holiday' in hospital. We are amazed and gratified to see the number of different people who give their time and gifts to these families, to try to bring some joy in their difficulties. The people that work on the day, when most of us are at home with our loved ones, do so generously and cheerfully.

Back home, we have a lovely morning, with many gifts, wonderful food and family. Late in the afternoon, after the kitchen has been tidied and contented weariness is beginning to overtake me, I head for a nap on the settee.

James stops me and pulls me to a quiet corner. I can tell he's afraid. I want to hide, to deny, to run away. He shows me a huge lump in the crease between his stump leg and his body. He tells me he's asked the doctor about it and has been assured that it's just his lymph system fighting the infection but he's not convinced himself.

I feel raw pain sear through the tender new skin of my being. Selfishly and irrationally, I am angry with James for keeping this from me and also for sharing it with me on this special day. Mostly, I feel a tremendous, crushing weight of dread.

*

Christmas has always been a cherished time for our family. Howard and I are not 'shoppers'. Most of my clothes have been gifts. If I do buy myself something, I'm always surprised and deeply disappointed when it wears out because then I have to go and find something else to replace it. To us 'Santa' is an opportunity to give in secret, purely for the joy of seeing the happiness your gift brings. We take a lot of time and trouble to think about the people we love and seek out the things that will meet their needs and/or bring them pleasure. Just as we are commanded to be the hands and feet of Jesus, we can also be the embodiment of St Nicholas. There really is a Santa Claus – we are he.

When James was born, Becky, my friend Janie's big sister, sent him a 'Night Before Christmas' book with moveable parts throughout the story. Every Christmas Eve we've cuddled up to read it before the boys have gone to bed, it's become part of our family tradition.

When the boys were small and money tight, we made many of their gifts. Howard has spent hours hiding in the loft or garage, restoring old bikes to make them like new or building things like his papier-mâché version of the wonderful 'Castle Greyskull' that doubled as a toy box to store their He-man figures. I made clothes, pyjamas, toys and even little wash kits. One year I made James a massive, fuzzy green dinosaur and David, a caveman. We wrap up new toothbrushes, batteries, sweets, bubble bath, everything, and with such a large family that all send presents, our Christmas tree looks like an island in a sea of brightly coloured parcels on Christmas morning. That's another thing; everything has to be hidden until the children are asleep, including our gifts to each other. It got much harder once they reached their teens to get them to go to bed before we fell asleep.

We had to confess to James when he started high school that we were, in fact, Father Christmas. He had defended the existence of Santa to all his friends, adamant that his parents could never have afforded all that we received.

I still get so excited I wake up several times in the night and am sometimes the first one up at 6 am, when we are allowed to phone the grandparents to come over. Howard insists that we all eat a good breakfast before we can open any gifts, which heightens the anticipation to fever pitch.

Chapter 4

As the extended family has grown, the tradition has evolved that we get together with Howard's brothers and sisters and families in the week after Christmas. This takes the hassle out of whose in-laws you visit each year and enables most of us to have Christmas in our own homes. We live roughly in the centre of the country for our relatives that live in Scotland and those who live near London. Howard's mum is nearby so in the days following Christmas, our home fills with visitors and James asks me not to share this new development with them.

I am staggered by his acting ability. He's as silly and fun-loving as always, sledging with the rest of the family, crutches and all, and having a great time. I have to look very closely to see the tight grip he has on himself.

The whole-body scans and tests are booked for my birthday. It snows all day but I manage to get James to the hospital in Leeds and Howard and David meet us at Meadowhall afterwards for a film, to celebrate. There is nowhere to eat so we end up driving back to Leeds for a meal. We're home by 8 pm because James has a party to go to.

Howard, David and I decide to take an evening walk along the cliffs above the Holme Valley and Pat, Jim and Lucy come along, too. It's magical. We're warm with walking in the deep sparkling snow, the lights below us twinkle and the children (including Howard) enjoy diving head first into the drifts.

James and I go back to hospital for his results. With a huge smile the doctor, a woman we've not come across before, informs us that the tests all show that James is clear. I *desperately* want to believe this confident professional. But James is still very unhappy about the lump in his groin. He presses her to assure him she's 100% certain it can't be cancer.

I trust my son and want him to know that I take his fears seriously, even if the different doctors seem to want to brush them aside. On the desk, in front of this doctor, is a bulging lever arch file with James' notes. I know from dealing with teaching records that too much information is impossible to read and consider. Often the important bits are missed.

'I think James is worried because the surgeon who performed the amputation phoned us with the pathology results on his leg.' I speak clearly in defence of my son. 'He said there was evidence that the small blood vessels and lymph nodes had been infiltrated by the cancer.'

The colour vanishes from the doctor's face and she flies out of the room. When she returns, she informs us that an appointment has been booked to remove the lymph gland the following week.

The new school term has started and I've returned to work so Howard takes James for this operation. The surgeon tells them it wasn't what he'd expected to find and he isn't happy with the colour of the lymph gland. We're to come back on Monday for the pathology results. The next day, Kenneth takes James for the first fitting of his new artificial leg.

I can't face going to school on Monday without knowing what the latest report will be, so Howard, James and I all sit silently, without breathing, in the doctor's office. The news is devastating. The gland was swollen with cancer and because it's come whilst James was having chemotherapy, it is chemical resistant. The doctor suggests a long shot – radical surgery to remove all the lymph nodes up James' stump and into his pelvis, right back to his kidneys. There are no guarantees that it will work or that the cancer isn't already in his blood. If it reappears, there is nothing left to try.

'You should consider carefully how you wish to spend what time you might have left with James.'

The doctor's words feel like a death sentence. My tongue has become a Velcro-covered radiator, air can barely get past into my gasping lungs. My vision flashes red and black, ghostly movements a long way away tell me I've left my body somehow. I phone my headmistress, who suggests I take the rest of the week off and let her know what's happening next, when we've had time to think.

Thinking isn't something I have much appetite for, especially at night, when worries grow into nightmares that start while I'm still awake. One thing that seems to still the fears enough for me to get some sleep, is reading the Bible. I reach for the tiny Gideon's version, that they hand out in high schools, and I'm directed to passages specific for my needs, a useful life belt for the drowning.

*

Not long after my mother died, I was home alone one day, when two middle-aged women appeared at the door and asked if they could speak to me. They were Jehovah's Witnesses and, as I was interested to know more about God, I invited them in. They spoke at length and left a stack of reading materials for me but I was deeply disturbed by the picture they painted of the God they believed in. It was not the loving Father of my limited experience, or the image I had grown up with, at all.

I looked up some of the quotes I'd been given and found they'd been lifted completely out of context and even reworded in parts. Who was right? Why were there so many different ways to worship one God? I decided to read the Bible, from the beginning, and try to see for myself what God was like, what He wanted. Regular Bible reading became part of my life. Even though sometimes my eyes would merely skim the page or the words would make little sense, occasionally a passage would 'light up' and I began to learn more about our Lord.

***

I go back onto long-term sick leave from work and slowly, slowly find my way back to life. James, as usual, leads the way with his calm certainty that the cancer will be out of his body after this next surgery. It suddenly occurs to me what a dreadful waste of life and hope it would be to grieve for a child who is still with me. I'm racing ahead of myself, embracing a doom that is not certain. After all, hadn't my own aunt been given a similar gloomy forecast for her demise, when both breasts and her lymph glands were removed more than 15 years earlier?

The next day, James takes possession of his new leg, at last. He adjusts to it as if it's just a different kind of shoe and it brings tears to my eyes to see him walking again. It's very heavy (so it won't blow away, apparently) and his muscles will need to grow stronger and the skin of his stump become tougher before he can wear the prosthesis all the time. He manages to wear it to a football match and is doing well with it before his next big operation, a week later.

We're on another ward in a different building in the hospital grounds for this surgery. The anaesthetist asks James what he's going to dream about during the operation.

'Beautiful women,' he replies with a grin.

The surgery lasts for three hours. Waiting doesn't get any easier with practice. The surgeon seems happy with how it's gone. James is only sick once afterwards but it's scary seeing him in the High Dependency Unit (HDU). He has an epidural tube coming out of his back, a catheter, two drains in the wound, a drip attached to his portacath and monitors on his chest and finger. It's extremely hot in the room with beeps, clicks and alarms going all the time. They keep him overnight but are forced to send him back onto the ward early because they need the beds. We aren't sorry, though, because it's so stifling and busy in the HDU we hope James will rest and recover more easily in the main ward.

The surgical ward is strikingly different to the oncology unit. The nurses don't get quite as involved because their patients are only transitory. They aren't trained to use the portacath so very kind nurses come over from the cancer unit to take blood, put in and take out needles, etc. We're very impressed by the number of oncology nurses who pop in just to visit and give James a cuddle. Howard smiles and teases him, when one young nurse comes to see James in the HDU, and the heart monitor betrays a steep rise in his blood pressure. On the plus side, the surgical ward is quieter and more relaxed than the oncology unit.

Browsing in the hospital shop for a treat for James, I meet the mother of another teenager from the cancer wards. Her son also has a tumour in his leg, which hasn't responded to treatment. They seem to be in denial. Her son refuses to even consider or discuss amputation and they feel they have to respect his decision. She's telling me something about his anxiety over acne. My heart goes out to her but I can't think of any words. I say a quick, silent prayer for this family and offer thanks for James' courage.

I learn a few days later that her son has died.

*

The first year, after my mother's death, plays across my memory. Every milestone had an aching resonance; birthdays, traditional family celebrations, personal victories previously shared and everyday bits of news. I found I couldn't bear other teenagers *complaining* about their mothers.

Somehow, despite our house move, Miss Loomis, my fifth grade teacher, heard about the tragedy and sent me a small book of poetry. I never had the opportunity to thank her but those poems have been very important to me ever since, as has the memory of her thoughtfulness. My favourite is this:

Immortality

Do not stand at my grave and weep…
I am not there. I do not sleep.

I am a thousand winds that blow,
I am the diamond glints on snow.
I am the sunlight on ripened grain,
I am the gentle autumn rain.
When you awake in the morning's hush,
I am the swift upflinging rush
Of quiet birds in circling flight.
I am the soft star-shine at night.

Do not stand at my grave and cry…
I am not there. I did not die.

Author Unknown

I came to realise that I didn't need to 'know' what had happened to my mother once she had gone. If this life was it, then she was now beyond pain or infirmity and she had used the life she'd been given well. If there were more, heaven or eternal life, then she would now be immersed in the pure love I had so far merely glimpsed. As for me, I choose not to go to her grave or remember dark dates, rather I enjoy a secret smile when a favourite song or event or even the reflection of my mother's hands, echoed in my own, bring a happy memory to mind.

Another poem, sent to me decades later by a mother who had just lost her twenty-one-year-old daughter, reflects a similar message.

You can shed tears that she is gone
Or you can smile because she has lived.

You can close your eyes and pray that she'll come back
Or you can open your eyes and see all she's left.

Your heart can be empty because you can't see her
Or you can be full of love you shared.

You can turn your back on tomorrow and live yesterday
Or you can be happy for tomorrow because of yesterday.

You can remember her and only that she's gone
Or you can cherish her memory and let it live on.

You can cry and close your mind, be empty and turn your back
Or you can do what she'd want: smile, open your eyes, love and go on.

Anonymous

***

The nurses seem very lax about administering drugs on the surgical ward. They don't appear to have the same careful handing-over procedures we've always seen in oncology. I tell them, when they're admitting James, that he's prone to constipation when given anaesthetics and/or painkillers so is usually given preventatives. The nurse writes this down in my presence and assures me she will have a prescription written up. A week later, it appears she's done nothing and James is in a very bad way. They are forced to give him much stronger laxatives, at this point, resulting in terrible stomach cramps and a desperate and difficult rush for the toilet.

Once the epidural is removed, the doctor instructs that James be given painkillers regularly and morphine for any breakthrough pain. But he only receives the ordinary painkillers when we remind the nurses. Slowly, James seems to improve each day over the week, until Tuesday when he dips again. Despite that, the doctor lets him go home on Wednesday because James is so desperate and I suggest he might recover better there.

Getting ready for bed James notices that his right testicle is swollen. He thinks it must be cancer again and decides not to tell us so we can have a worry free night. The next morning, I can't untangle my feelings about this. I'm anxious about what else he might keep from us, yet overwhelmed by his bravery and thoughtfulness, coping with such a fear alone.

I rush him back to hospital, where we see three different doctors at various stages in their training. James is all for them cutting him open again, to make sure, and the doctors all look disconcertedly uncertain of what to do. When I suggest using ultrasound (drawing on my own experience with the breast lump) the doctor replies in relief, 'Oh, that's a good idea.' They decide the inflammation is epididymitus (whatever that is), not cancer, and send us home again with some antibiotics.

On Friday, we're back at the hospital for the results of the pathology report following the lymph node surgery. We wait hours, with my heart pounding, mouth dry and hands wet, in the children's oncology outpatients unit. The sickly sour smell of disease, medicine and bodily fluids makes the air thick and difficult to breathe. There is no comfort in the pink plastic-coated furniture, toys, bright picture-covered walls or children with haunted parents.

The atmosphere in the consulting room is sombre. The doctor's folded arms, the set of his eyebrows and even the lighting seem determined to eliminate any possible spark of false hope. We're told that there had been some cancer where the diseased lymph node had been situated but the whole of the area has been removed and the borders appear clear. Miraculously, the rest of the lymph nodes appear to be clear, as well. We're told to return in three weeks (then monthly after that) for a chest x-ray and check-up. Seemingly, if the cancer is in his blood, it will turn up in his lungs next.

The doctor suggests that James and I go down to the labs and look at some of James' cancer cells under the microscope. What we see is bizarre; cells of wildly different, irregular shape and size with huge variations in the contents of the nuclei. They are constantly mutating, with a variety of chromosomes (up to 70). The doctors have never seen anything like it. This phenomenon probably explains why some of the cells were destroyed and some weren't and why it's been so hard to treat. It's not unusual for cancers in teenagers to break the rules.

Early on, we promised James we would take him, and some of his friends, on a special holiday anywhere he wanted to go, when he was well enough. This was by way of giving him a dream, something to look forward to and focus on. The consultant knows about this and suggests we consider going on the trip sooner rather than later, implying there might not be a later. But James is adamant that he is now clear of the cancer. He is determined that we will go on the holiday in the summer, when he and his friends have finished their big exams and high school.

It is frightening to ignore the advice of a doctor and believe instead in the opinion of a sixteen-year-old. But this is James' body and it's his call. He is my son and I must stand by him.

*

My mom knew me like that, too. When I was ten and uncharacteristically terrified of going back to school at the end of the summer, she patiently winkled the story out of me. Living near the primary school, we local children used to play there on the swings and other equipment. One day the school caretaker asked us if we wanted to come into the building to play hide-and-seek. We thought this was a great idea and felt wildly naughty being in the school when no-one else was there. We ran in the polished corridors and even peeked in the boys' toilets.

My heart pounded with uncertainty when this faded, heavy-set man suggested a good hiding place. I didn't know how to say no to adults, especially one who had been kind to my friends and me. When the fireproof door sealed us in the thumping boiler room, he tried to force himself on me. In a terrified frenzy, I managed to wriggle out of his sweaty grasp and escape. I felt so frightened and ashamed. I couldn't bring myself to tell anyone what had happened until my Mom reassured me. As far as I know, the man had disappeared so I didn't have to go through any police or court experiences.

***

James doesn't seem to be recovering at home after the surgery, as we had expected. By Saturday, he isn't able to eat any breakfast and when he tries to eat some lunch, he brings it back up. I phone the hospital and they suggest we get the GP to have a look at him. One of our wonderful doctors comes out straight away and gives him six packets of Dioralyte, an electrolyte powder to replace body salts and sugar. He's to drink them all between now and Sunday morning when the doctor will come back to have another look at him. It's like a miracle; James begins to look better after the first one.

The GP isn't happy about the epididymitus diagnosis, though, and sends us to a specialist in Huddersfield on Monday. The consultant tells James he is certain it isn't anything to do with cancer; it's just fluid in the sack. It could get even bigger and will probably take some time to go away. He offers to aspirate to make him more comfortable but James isn't keen. He will be seeing the surgeon on Wednesday for his follow-up appointment and could return to the specialist at the end of January, if necessary.

Months before James started being poorly, Howard had told me about two friends at work who'd been to a 'healer', with remarkable results. Suddenly, for no apparent reason, this story comes into my mind. I carefully read the man's book to try to reassure myself that we wouldn't be doing anything against God, if we go to see him. In the book, the man doesn't claim any credit for the healings he's been involved in but attributes them to some higher being working through him. The Bible is full of stories of healing; why shouldn't God still work through people in this way?

I wonder if it might help and, determined not to have any 'what ifs', I suggest to James we give it a go. Howard's been having trouble with his knees, which often glow red hot and are very painful. James agrees to this latest crazy notion of mine, if his dad will also go. They both think I'm gaga but consent, if only to humour me. I phone and make an appointment.

We search the dark, quiet back streets of a Bradford suburb to find the healer's house. The building's large and Victorian. Our tyres scrunch on gravel lit by a porch light. Inside, it's old fashioned and fussy and makes me think of grannies. The foyer is clean but there's a faint smell of damp and possibly cats. We're shown into a dimly-lit sitting-room and I perch on the edge of a vinyl settee. The man shuffles in and is more than 70 years old, slightly stooped with lush silver hair.

He speaks softly and has Howard sit on a low stool in the centre of the small room. His hands hover over Howard's head and spine, whilst he asks questions about lifestyle and pain patterns. He has Howard stand, walk and bend over. The man explains that Howard's spine is slightly out of line, which causes an imbalance that puts strain on his knees. He then rests his hands on several places on Howard's body and seems to look inside himself.

Almost without a sound James and Howard change places. Whilst the man lays his hands on James, he affirms what James has been telling us, he can't feel the presence of any more disease in my son.

I find this place and the gentle wash of words soothing and reassuring. It's as if a tap has been turned on inside me and cleansing tears just flow quietly the whole time. When the healer has ministered to Howard and James, he sits lightly beside me and murmurs a few tender words. My tears are stilled and my insides rest. Howard's knees are ice-cold and pain-free (a condition that lasts for many months afterwards). We barely speak on the way home but it's an easy silence.

*

During my second summer at university, I took some extra classes in the spring term then arranged to go on a social sciences course in England through July and August. It was a fantastic opportunity. The first two weeks ·we stayed in student accommodation at a London university. We were given 'go-as-you-please' tube passes and encouraged to see as much as we could. I made friends with a wonderful, scatty art student called Deborah and we explored to our hearts' content. There were also lectures and organised visits to places like Stonehenge, the Houses of Parliament, Brighton, and Coventry Cathedral. A young, local girl I met invited me to tea in her home and I shared a very pleasant afternoon with her family.

From London we moved to the beautiful, ancient student rooms in Oriel College, Oxford, for a month. I fell in love with the creamy old stone, smooth green quadrangles, colourful window boxes and dark timbers. It was living history. We learned about the British government, economy, health service, education, social services and media, all aspects of society.

One day, we visited a local primary school and I was very impressed by the creativity, freedom and pleasure of the children and staff. They had one of those large temporary pools with rigid sides and the children were having swimming lessons in the sunlit, leafy-green, playground. Their library was full of books the children had made alongside the more conventional store-bought variety. That particular visit was to have life-changing consequences for me, as it was the reason I chose to do my final teaching practice in Yorkshire.

Over a long weekend, Deborah and I hired a car, with two more friends, and drove all the way to Ullapool, Scotland, stopping in the Lake District and generally taking in the wide variety of landscapes. I particularly loved the green and mauve moors with their endless, rambling stone walls. I tried to imagine the folk who built them in such remote places. It was so exhilarating to run up the side of a mountain after hours in the car and later to feel the northern salty air on our faces as we peered out across Loch Broom towards the Outer Hebrides.

The final two weeks we travelled across Europe by train, visiting Paris, Lucerne, Florence, Venice, Rome and Frankfurt. We stayed in clean, simple bed and breakfasts, soaking up the sunshine, variety and beauty of these fascinating places. It was such a blessing to have Deborah as a companion, to see it all through her artistic gaze, as she paused to sketch anything that took her fancy.

My friend had been scarred by a difficult and painful childhood. Back in the USA, Deborah became a 'born again' Christian. I remember her coming to my parents home and talking to them about Jesus, hoping to help them. She also took me to her evangelistic church, where people spoke in tongues, writhed on the floor and other things I'd not experienced before. I found both events embarrassing and threatening but I could see the radiant joy in my wounded friend and was grateful to God that he'd found a way to reach her. The perfect Father, it seems, has a variety of methods to meet the needs of his very different children.

***

Tuesday the fourth of February is the first day for a long time that James doesn't have to see a doctor. He balances on his crutches in the kitchen, rocking his body back and forth with his toe against the worktop. Laughing, he teases David, who grumbles his reply from the bedroom. There is pink and warmth in his skin. His eyes sparkle with mischief beneath their new ruff of dark lashes and the curve of his returning eyebrows. I brush my hand against his velvety hair, stronger now the first weak new growth has been shaved. He ducks away from me, spins and bounces off, racing his brother out the door and up the lane to collect Jim.

The people in his school have been wonderful. The headmaster's come to our home to offer his support on more than one occasion. In the English school system, the final two years of high school (14 to 16 year olds) are devoted to quite intense study, which culminates in some very important coursework and exams, known as GCSEs. The results of these will determine whether, and where, students can continue to study and are a factor universities consider when offering them a place, after they complete two further years of 'A-level' work in a sixth-form college.

James, whilst struggling to attend as often as possible, has missed a great deal of time in school. Physics, in particular has suffered, because the practical two-hour session is held on Monday afternoons. Every third Monday James was too ill, following chemotherapy, to attend and for the three weeks of his radiotherapy he missed every afternoon. Added to this is the time spent in surgery and recovery.

We're also concerned about his French studies, as there's only so much he can learn on his own from the textbook and conversation tapes. He isn't having enough opportunity to practice speaking the language. A friend recommended a local tutor and she's fantastic with James, especially in building his confidence.

Receiving the school reports for our boys, we are proud beyond words. David is now playing saxophone in the Senior Wind Band and Big Band (jazz), editor of the school newspaper and doing well in every class. This is a quote from James' report:

The commitment that James has obviously shown towards his work this year should serve as an inspiration to all of us. Straight A's for effort across the range reflects his determination to do well, his mature attitude and spirited personality have made him such a popular student with both staff and pupils alike. I am sure that his dedication will earn him the GCSE grades he seeks and the admiration of us all.

Howard is beginning to feel a bit happier in his job but is still working extremely hard and putting in long hours. We're now living under the threat that the Bradford offices will be closed within the next twelve months and we will be expected to move to Stratford-upon-Avon. Taking James from the medical team that have supported him so well, moving the boys into new schools at this critical time in their studies and trying to find a new job for me, after long-term sick leave, seem like insurmountable obstacles. Never mind leaving our support network of local family, friends and church.

I recall Howard's mum sitting beside me one Sunday during one of the many deep dips in James' treatment. I could feel the tension in her body. Her stiff-upper-lip, keep-feelings-private social mask was under tremendous pressure. The congregation had just prayed for us. She gripped my arm, with fear in her face. 'I can't bear it, Kimm, I can't bear it,' she whispered. How could we leave her?

*

I had been drawn by the closeness of Howard's family and stability of the community, and then his siblings all married 'foreigners' and moved away, apart from Louise who married a local man. Delith emigrated to the homeland of her Australian opera-singing husband. Lorraine's Chris is a 'southerner', once in the RAF, and they live in Scotland. Matthew married a gorgeous Welsh singer and lives in London, as does his youngest brother, Simeon, and his beautiful 'southern' wife. My brothers on the other hand continue to live in the area we'd grown up in and are in business with my dad.

When Howard had been four months in his new job, after the redundancy, his father died. Geoffrey had been to London to celebrate his sixtieth birthday and came back looking grey. He hated hospitals and resisted going but there was nothing else to be done. He'd been on borrowed time since having a serious heart attack four years earlier. Howard stayed with him through his final night and came home heartbroken. Our little boys couldn't understand our tears or why they couldn't see their granddad. We quickly realised our blessing in Howard's new boss, Darrell, who understood and supported the idea that family must come before work.

With Geoffrey's death, it was our turn to support Mum. She was in the midst of trying to sell her big house, a process begun during Geoffrey's incapacity. The stress of joining 'chains' of buyers and sellers then having those chains fall apart added to the agonies of bereavement. Trials seem to come in clusters; within a relatively short period Mum also lost her only brother and her beloved stepmum, then her daughter and one of her grandchildren moved to the other side of the world. At least Simeon still lived at home, working on his A-levels, so she wasn't alone.

Eight months after being widowed, Mum finally managed to sell her house and it was time to say goodbye to the place she'd lived in for 22 years. To make it easier, she moved in with us. She would then be a cash buyer, once she found a house she liked. We called her our 'Granny in the Attic'. Matthew and Simeon came, as well, until they went off to university in the autumn. By selling her large, rambling home she was able to buy a much smaller, semi-detached house with a nice garden and lovely neighbour and still have a significant amount of money to invest. This would supplement her pathetic state pension when she retired.

Life was hectic for her. She still worked full time, as a mender in the woollen mill, two of her daughters were expecting babies, she was planning a solo visit to Australia in March and Matthew's wedding would be in April. The house she eventually found and bought needed quite a bit of work done on it, so we rolled up our sleeves and lent a hand. She lived with us for about nine months.

Many people warned us that living together might put a great strain on our relationships but we didn't find that at all. Only David struggled to share his mum during meals. We had some terrible battles over food at teatime. It took us a while to realise that, apart from the exhaustion of just starting playschool, he was upset because I was focussing my attention on his grandma, talking about her day, and not on him.

Howard's mum continued to attend her church in Holmfirth, which had a crèche and Sunday school classes so the boys and I began to go along with her on occasion. I also started helping on the Thursday morning coffee rota again. Howard would come to church with us sometimes but it wasn't for him.

Even though we were nearby and saw Mum regularly, living alone was hard for her. When Kenneth swept Mum off her feet nine years after Geoffrey's death, we couldn't have been happier for them both.

***

Howard and I decide to book a weekend away for Valentines Day. We realise we're taking a chance because it's already early February but we receive the paperwork just in time. There seems to be a minor error so we double-check before we set off on Saturday and are assured that everything is all right.

However, when we arrive after a long drive, there is no room for us. The manager asks us to wait in the bar whilst they try to sort something out. I flop into a chair, as limp and wrinkled as the linen trousers I'm wearing.

Eventually we're offered a room, which is so tiny I can only stand up in half of it. There's only one cup, towel, dressing gown, etc and we've paid for a suite. The manager tells us that our meal that night will be extra special to make up for the inconvenience.

It's a lovely hotel with a tree house large enough for family parties in the summer. There are dressing up clothes, a den, tiny kitchen and a real Enid Blyton feel to it. We can just imagine our extended family having a wonderful time there. But Howard, in desperate need of a restful break, can't relax all afternoon, convinced we will be invited to eat on a fold-up table in the corridor.

As it turns out, we have a terrific meal, at a proper table in the posh restaurant. There's an excellent pianist, tasteful decor and the sea-rhythm murmur of contented conversation. We're sound asleep in our miniscule room by 10pm.

*

When I look back through my memories, it's often the holidays and special times that stand out. The routines of every day fade. Howard feels the same so we've always given priority to trips away, even when money was short. There's something about a shared adventure, uninterrupted by mitments, chores, work or even other family and friends that strengthens the fibres of our relationships.

Howard is a master at holiday planning but occasionally I have a go. The birthday surprise I organised for Howard, just before James was born, had echoes in the Valentine fiasco. I'd wanted us to have a romantic weekend alone together, while it was still just the two of us, but I never could resist a bargain.

When we finally found the ancient static caravan, in a field on some remote farm in Wales, we wondered why the lights were so dim. On closer inspection we discovered they were up-lighters and three-quarters full of dead bugs. The outdoor shower block – and this was October – was full of giant snails. Heavily pregnant and exhausted by baby preparations, we slept through the weekend then, as well. So much for romance.

***

As James improves, I am again faced with going back to work. This time, I'm frightened, almost superstitious. Once you've had three months or more out of the classroom with a stress-related illness, you could be a danger to children or yourself so must be cleared by local authority doctors. I've nearly reached the 100-day limit for receiving full pay and need to return. Fortunately, the doctors clear me and I go back to school for a week before the February half-term holiday. This gives me a chance to get used to being at work, assess the children and plan more accurately for the coming weeks.

During the holiday, I take James for his monthly cancer check-up. For two weeks prior to this, I can feel pressure building up in my chest. I wake earlier and earlier each day, between 3 and 5 am, unable to get back to sleep or lie still or concentrate. My breathing is short and shallow. I get through my days a moment at a time.

At the clinic, we queue for a slip of paper, which we take to another building where we queue for x-rays. We wait in a corridor with others in pain, resigned, afraid. There are elderly people laid on trolleys, children, a woman in flowing clothes of bright fuchsia, carefully embroidered. Illness cares nothing for age or race, gender or religion.

From there we return to the clinic and wait again, this time to get the results and speak to the doctor. The familiar pink plastic furniture, smells and news of other children amplify the adrenalin I can feel burning round my twitching muscles. My body is pumped up tight.

The doctor tells us James' lungs are clear, he'll see us again in a month. Relief, euphoria and deflation slam through me in quick succession. The fight-or-flight chemicals switch off and I'm suddenly so weary, I can barely walk out to the car. It takes a week for the wrung-out feeling to dissipate.

I am surprised by the similarity to the flatness I feel after Christmas. Then the build up, preparation and anticipation culminate in the big celebration. Despite all the lovely gifts and pleasant memories, I often feel sad when the day is over. This should have been the opposite. It was dread and fear that lead up to the results. James has stayed clear of cancer for a month. This is the best of all possible outcomes. I should be dancing. But the roller coaster exhausts me and I am wary of another ambush. I curl around this good news and keep my head down.

Back at work, the head teacher receives notice that we will have our first ever OFSTED inspection in the next school year. The inspections are very rigorous and, being fairly new, rumour and horror stories proliferate. A team of people will come into our school for a whole week, having first reviewed all the policies and planning. They will examine displays and resources, talk to children and parents, watch everyone teach several lessons throughout the week and members of the senior management team will have intense, individual interviews.

My head teacher comes into my classroom shortly after this news is announced to the staff. She asks me if I will consider giving up my senior management position for a year. She says she's concerned that I am under enough stress at home and the additional burden of the inspection at senior level might be too much. Part of me is offended and very angry that OFSTED should be able to have such an impact on my life. It's supposed to make teachers more accountable and I have no objection to anyone looking at my work. I always try to do my best whether anyone is watching or not.

After all we've been through; it feels so unfair to be asked to give up my hard- won position and possible future promotion. I'd completed one module towards a Master's Degree and still hoped to become a deputy head teacher one day. I talk to friends, family and colleagues, even my union. I pray, worry and try to consider all the 'what if's.

In spite of this, the intensity of teaching is just what I need. Not only is there relief from imminent financial worries but my days are spent absorbed in the care of others.

*

The school I teach in is multicultural and nearly half the children come from families with different cultural backgrounds and often languages other than English are spoken in their homes.

In the year before James became ill, my head teacher suggested I might like to take part in a Multilingual Achievement Partnership project. There was an optional opportunity to attend extra night classes at the university to complete the first module of a Master's Degree, which I decided to take. I found the action research based on the work I was doing in my classroom, the lectures, meetings and extra reading, gave me a new energy and enthusiasm. The extra course work, teaching year two children, with the added pressures of SATs (Standardised Achievement Tests) and my additional management responsibilities kept me very busy.

As part of this project, I was one of four people asked to do a presentation of my work to the other sixty participants. Being very nervous about this, I tried to ensure I was fully prepared for the big event. The night before, I retired early in order to be fresh and relaxed for the coming day. My hair always sculpts itself in weird and wonderful ways, if I sleep on it damp so I planned to wash it in the morning. I'd been asleep for about an hour when I was woken by Howard's shouts.

He'd decided the central heating boiler needed some adjustment. It's situated in a cupboard in the spare bedroom so on his way to bed from the bathroom, he started tinkering with it.

I found him with his bare bottom in the air under the boiler with water spraying everywhere. I managed to turn the water off at the mains but we were unable to fix the problem. This meant that waking from a poor night's sleep, I had to brush my teeth with water siphoned from the de-humidifier and beg my friend to let me wash my hair at her house when I arrived to collect her for the seminar. There's something about rushing in slightly late to give a presentation with wet hair that allows you to abandon all thoughts of making a good impression.

***

James sees quite a few different doctors at the end of February and is passed fit by all of them, thankfully. We are invited to Sheffield to watch the Para Olympic track team training. It's reassuring and humbling to see these dedicated people overcome every obstacle. James still isn't able to wear his prosthesis (artificial leg) yet, following his surgery, but that doesn't stop him joining in for an hour and a half's aerobics on one leg. The organisation hopes to have 2000 athletes to compete in the 2000 Olympics in Australia; an exciting possibility.

At home, James sticks to the demanding exercise routine for a while but doesn't appear to be as keen as we are for him to take up this challenge. He has a heavy load of commitments already and perhaps can't face taking on one more.

The first weekend in March, we travel to London to share in our niece's dedication. This is a little bit like a christening, in the Baptist church. It's fantastic to visit with our larger family, as well as taking in the sights of the capital city, a trip to the theatre and some nice meals. The following Sunday is Mothering Sunday and David, toying with the idea of becoming an atheist, finds himself in church for the second week running.

A week later, we take friends with us to watch a mutual acquaintance perform in an amateur operatic version of *South Pacific*. It's great fun and we have a lovely evening until we return to the car park and discover the car isn't there. It's a very odd feeling to have your car stolen. We walk up and down all the rows several times before we can actually believe it. At least no one was hurt. We're with friends, who need to get home, so we phone the police and get a taxi.

Two days later, at 5:50 am, we're woken with a sickening start by a phone call from the police. They tell us our car has been abandoned, in the middle of a busy street in the centre of Leeds, without any wheels. We're asked to ·move it immediately, as it's causing an obstruction and they think the thieves might return to burn it out.

Our sleep-fuzzed minds aren't sure how to do that from forty minutes' drive away at that hour but, thankfully, the AA manage to move it to a garage for us and Howard's insurance company delivers a hire car to our home by the afternoon. James has another clear cancer check that same day and compared to that, a stolen car seems inconsequential.

Gradually, life begins to become more normal. For Howard's fortieth birthday present, I engaged a gardener to design and landscape our small weed-ridden eyesore of a vegetable patch. Now that spring is here, he's able to turn his drawings into reality. We feel able to go out more with friends again, to the cinema, for walks, etc and our various work commitments occupy more of our thoughts. We start to plan in earnest for the special summer holiday James wants in America.

*

The agreement we made with my family in the US, when Howard and I got married, was that we would try to visit them every other year, if possible, and my parents would visit us in the alternate years. This has worked out very well. What we've lost in frequency we've made up for in intensity of time spent together.

In our early years of marriage, my family would often send money to help us with our air fares. Once we were in America, my relatives would put us up, feed, entertain and drive us about. It was often cheaper to go there than to a holiday spot in Europe. When the boys were in junior school they once complained about having to go to the States all the time because all their friends got to go camping in France.

On these biannual visits, everyone would make an effort to see us, often taking time off from their lives. For years I also wrote regular long newsy letters, which I photocopied then added individual notes on the bottom. These I sent to my relatives in America and to Howard's siblings. We hadn't realised how our visits and letters had enabled us to remain close as a family, despite the distance, until Howard and I were looking at houses. We knocked on the door of a possible purchase only to discover one of Howard's cousins lived there. I didn't recognise her. It was clear that Howard knew my cousins and what they were up to better then we knew his.

For their first visit, my dad and Nicki brought both my brothers and my stepsister and hired a camper van for the boys to sleep in. James hadn't been born yet, so we just about managed to accommodate everyone. The second time my parents brought my grandma and I can still hear her saying 'No-nee, no-nee' to James, who took his first steps for her, while she babysat. I was quite jealous about that.

Over the years we've had many brilliant holidays with my family in five different states and Canada. Weddings have been planned so that we could be there. Our boys have been able to try skiing, visit Disneyworld, canoe in the midst of alligators, experience the log cabin of my summers and see a baseball game amongst other experiences.

For various reasons, I hadn't been able to go to either of my beloved grandmothers' funerals. It feels horribly unreal and isolating to be bereaved from a distance. There's no one around you to share your memories or loss. When you are away from people you love, they somehow stay the same in your mind, like a photo. It's always surprising to visit my family and find they have gone on without me. In my grandmothers' particular 'photos' in my mind, they're still there, in the homes I remember from my childhood.

I can understand how hard it must have been for my family to read in my letters about James' illness, treatment and surgeries. They need to see us, to wrap us in the love they long to share. This holiday we're planning is important for all of us.

***

James is finally cleared to start wearing his artificial leg again, eight weeks after his surgery. It's a painful process, as he has to build up calluses where people don't normally have them and his leg muscles haven't been used for so long they are terribly weak. Like any teenager, James resists listening to advice from adults and hasn't been doing the exercises or wearing the shrink stocking designed to prepare his stump. He also finds it tedious having to build up his strength by wearing the prosthesis for gradually longer periods of time each day.

A week after he starts using it they take it off him, again. Seemingly, the end of his bone has become attached to the muscle and is causing him a lot of pain. The doctor decides that James needs a different kind of prosthesis. He has to push his stump into the old socket but would be pulled into the new one. With massage and some sort of ultra-sonic pulsar machine, they manage to free the muscle again. James doesn't like the new leg because it makes embarrassing wind noises from time to time, when he sits down, but hopefully it will only be temporary.

We go to pick the new leg up and discover James' hip is swollen. With alarm bells ringing, we rush back to oncology. Nothing is found and eventually the swelling goes back down. We'd been told, in October, that the sooner amputees can start using their prosthesis the better. The longer they're without, the stump bone thins, muscles atrophy and the other joints begin to twist to compensate for the shift in weight bearing, bringing risk of permanent damage. Finally, by the middle of March, James begins to use his leg, nearly five months after the amputation.

Two weeks later, it's the Easter holidays. Monday is glorious. Howard works in his garden all day and I enjoy a twelve-mile walk with friends. We flop into bed early and sink quickly into blissful sleep.

A heart-piercing scream wakes us in the still dark of deep night. We find James in a crumpled heap, shivering uncontrollably and panting very rapidly. We cover him and, stamping down our own panic, try to keep him calm. The ambulance seems to take ages but actually arrives quickly.

Getting up in the night to use the toilet, James had slipped. He'd twisted round, tried to grab the towel rail, which broke under his weight and fell awkwardly on his stump.

The doctor in casualty tells Howard that the hip is broken and will probably need to be pinned; the alternative is six weeks in hospital, in bed. James is admitted and Howard comes home.

I arrive early the next day in order to be present when the doctors do their rounds. Two 'under-doctors' appear and stand between James and I, with their backs to me, and seem unable or unwilling to answer any of my questions. I'm told the consultant will arrive about 1pm so Howard comes to hear what he has to say, as well.

This slim, greying man steams into the room, white coat billowing with his minions in his wake, and announces that pinning is no good for amputees. He orders more x-rays, makes a comment about James having two good arms and a good leg so he'll be OK. Once mobility is determined and pain relief under control, he can go home, we're told. Unfortunately, the consultant doesn't want to explain what he means or answer any questions and promptly disappears. We wait all day and at teatime we're told the x-ray department can't fit us in so we'll have to wait until tomorrow.

At least James seems to be all right. On Monday night he'd been very upset that something else had happened to him but he's back to his old self again. He's on morphine for the pain, which makes him very sleepy, but he seems to move about the bed fairly comfortably.

The next day, we're summoned to x-ray at 9 am only to be met by the man who'd taken the x-rays on Monday night. He spends forty minutes trying to find out why James needs more pictures of the same area. I tell him I certainly don't want James exposed to any more radiation than is absolutely necessary. We decide not to have the x-rays done and return to the ward. Late in the afternoon the nurse tells us that the consultant will be in theatre all day and might come to see us around 5pm if his operation doesn't run over.

I'm feeling quite angry and frustrated by this time. We're used to consultants who go out of their way to talk to us, answer our questions and involve us in decisions. As a parent, I need to know what we should be doing. Will James be bed-ridden for weeks or should we organise physiotherapy? Is it safe to take him swimming and would that help strengthen his muscles? How soon can we expect him to be able to use his artificial leg again? What will the pain management involve, when will James be able to switch to over-the-counter type relief? Are they giving him anything to prevent constipation? When will it be safe for him to return to school? I have lots of basic questions. I phone James' doctors at the other hospitals, to try to get some information, and they are as helpful as they are able to be without access to James or his medical notes.

Later, our brilliant friend, Pat, drops in to visit us. She just happens to be a member of the Community Health Council, a voluntary organisation of professional people that act as a watchdog for the health service. I let off steam about our experiences, amongst other things, and then she leaves to return to work. Shortly afterwards, the nurse rushes in to say the consultant is on his way. Pat had gone directly to the hospital administrator and the consultant's secretary, to complain about our treatment.

He is not pleased that the x-rays haven't been taken, nor I suspect that he'd been expected to see us. I have to follow him out of the room to try to get him to answer all of my questions. He tells me his junior doctor will look at the x-rays and, if they're OK, we can go. The x-ray department stays open an extra 15 minutes and rushes us right through.

The younger doctor is much nicer this time and shows us the pictures, talks us through the situation and explains what's going on. James has a spiral crack just below the sticky-out bits at the top of his femur. Being an amputee, there is nothing pulling on the bone and he isn't putting any weight through it so they hope an operation won't be necessary. He has to be very careful and they will check in two weeks to make sure the crack isn't spreading. Hopefully, it'll mend by itself. Thanks to Pat, we're home by Wednesday night with a clearer idea of what we should be doing and what to expect. The only difficulty is James' inability to comprehend the words 'rest' and 'careful'.

*

My son inherited these qualities from his granddad. When James was a baby, Howard's dad suffered a serious heart attack, which meant that he couldn't drive and was invalided off work. Heart disease was a feature of the family; Geoffrey had already lost two brothers to it. He'd been made redundant in the past, worked at a number of jobs and in his late fifties was a progress chaser in a local factory. Unemployment at that time was very high and he and his colleagues had lived under the constant threat of redundancy over a number of years. His vegetarian, non-smoking, teetotal lifestyle and low weight all helped him to live longer than his brothers but I believe it was that extra anxiety that pushed his heart beyond the limit.

Geoffrey was useless at being an invalid. Against medical advice and in the face of his family's anguish, he was soon steaming through life at nearly full blast. Gently, he helped each of us to understand that it wasn't quantity of life that was important but the quality. He had to be the person we loved and we couldn't deny him that. So we just held our breath when he went to entertain at a children's birthday party, took a part in a play or sped off on some other project.

Chapter 5

James is due for his next monthly check-up and I realise I am trapped in a cycle of nervous build-up then the exhausted relief afterwards. Going back to work for that first half term had felt like riding a push bike up Holme Moss; a lot of strenuous effort, slow progress and no coasting. The trauma of our Easter holiday has left me more shattered then I'd been when we broke up from school. I agree to give up my management responsibilities and accept the demotion.

The boys are in the thick of 'exam' season. David is taking mock (practice) GCSEs and James the real thing. We have fun and games trying to get the doctor in charge of his fracture to agree with the doctor in charge of his prosthesis. His stump is painful and we're told he has osteoporosis in the bone, making it more susceptible to fractures. This will be reversed if he can start using his leg.

Howard is working extremely hard, sometimes until 11:30 pm then up again at 5 am. He enjoys working as part of a team of men his own age and of like ability but I am concerned about the level of stress he's under. He's away more often than ever and it seems certain he will have to live in Stratford, at least a few days a week. We just can't see how the rest of us can move at this time but it's equally hard for him to be on his own and we miss having him around.

We are guests at his new boss's wedding in late spring. It's a second wedding for Alan but the bride's first. She's 36 years old and a successful businesswoman herself so they really go over the top. The service is held in a lovely old church and the minister must be 6'5" tall, with flowing, flaming red hair. He breathes in through his nose very loudly, long and deep, each time he begins to speak. His sermon is very sincere and from the heart but some people squirm and appear to be embarrassed.

The bride's dress is a stunning deep red and gold, in rich brocade material, and her bridesmaids are in pink brocade dresses cut like regal pageboys;

very appropriate for a reception held in a castle. The bridal couple are taken there in a royal blue, stretched limousine complete with two doormen and motorcycle outriders all dressed in matching blue uniforms, gold buttons and epaulets. The castle belongs to the seventh Earl of Caernarvon. The fifth Earl had been one of the explorers who had discovered the tomb of Tutankhamen so we also have a private tour of some of the artefacts after dinner. Despite all the pageantry, it's a lovely affair, warm, friendly and lots of fun.

I remember my own wedding, simple and relatively inexpensive. My grandma bought my wedding dress in a sale and we had the reception in my Dad's house. But the marriage is surely the point of it all and I hoped this couple would, together, find the strength to face the challenges life brings.

I'm beginning to have a real 'crossroads' feeling. In my head, I know I have to give James more space and try to find more focus in my own life. James' illness put an end to the idea of continuing with the Master's Degree. At school, I feel restless, again in need of a change. I'd always fantasised about being an author so start a correspondence course.

At church, I'm invited to join a worship team. Four or five of us from the congregation meet with the minister and plan a whole service. We start with the three readings from the Bible recommended for the week. At the first meeting we look at the verses, pray and generally brainstorm our ideas. I wake in the night with my head buzzing. The three readings link like puzzle pieces and I find the Spirit has inspired me to write a whole mini-sermon. When we meet again, the rest of the group make a few modifications, choose some hymns, a story for the children's address, prepare prayers and we're ready.

It's an incredibly uplifting experience. Several people encourage me to undertake the training and become a lay preacher. I'm honoured at being asked and excited by the possibility but Howard is deeply unhappy about it. He doesn't attend church regularly and neither do most of our friends, colleagues or acquaintances. I suspect he's worried by their reactions but also that the church would 'swallow' me up as it had his father. I made promises

before God, when I married this complicated man, so realise this isn't a path
He wants me to take.

*

I continued to go to church fairly regularly, since accompanying Mum
when she'd come to live with us. Our new home was within walking distance
of the place the family had always attended. I felt it was important for the
children to go to Sunday school. It was pleasant and the people were friendly
but I didn't feel a compulsion to be there. Until one Sunday, when the
minister, Mr Stocks, came up to me and said he wanted me to speak in the
Harvest service for five minutes. He then walked off without waiting for
my reply, not that I was capable of speaking at that point. The subject given
was the type of world I would like to see for myself and my children, as a
Christian.

In the Methodist church, ministers are moved on to another church every
five years or so. It must be very hard on them and their families but I think
it's quite stimulating for the churches. Mr Stocks was special. He would
infuriate me with 'throw away' statements in his sermons, which would
make me go home and try to work out why they made me feel that way. It
was a great way to get me to think more deeply about what I believed and
why. One Sunday, he said the Bible shouldn't be read from cover to cover
and I challenged him on that. His gentle smile only deepened at my passion.

This was something else entirely. I was completely at home speaking to a hall
full of children but standing up in front of a room full of adults and airing my beliefs
was terrifying. The process of praying, researching, planning and practising what I
was going to say, took weeks and changed the way I felt about church forever. I was
experiencing the power of God at a time when I was neither at the peak or the depths
of life's roller coaster and it was fantastic.

***

We're late. I misjudged the traffic and forgot to allow time to locate
a parking place in this unfamiliar corner of Leeds. Nowhere is flat in the
Pennines and in my smart shoes and skirt I half run uphill, beside James, to

the church. He can move very quickly on his crutches but his skin is flushed, as mine must be, in the May heat.

The hearse is just pulling up and we're able to slip into the cool dark of a pew near the back. The chill I feel goes deeper than the damp film on my skin. The church is full. Almost half are teenaged pupils from Foluso's school. Today they are children, bewildered and hurt. I glance at James. His face is grim. Hard set, it is a man's face.

The coffin seems too small. Foluso's name is spelt in flowers along the top. A smiling school photo looks out at us. He would have been fifteen today.

Agnes comes in surrounded by her family and my heart breaks. The words of the service wash over me, my thoughts circle and crash. Her shoes are too close and even the idea of being in them has my insides kicking and screaming.

It takes some time for us all to file out of the church. Each person offers a word or a touch to the family standing outside the doors. The similarity with a wedding reception line strikes me as grotesque, yet we need this opportunity to share a burden of pain, as much as sharing the gift of joy, with those who care.

Waiting my turn to speak, I can see Agnes and admire her strength. Stepping forward, she is suddenly in my arms and I can feel the grief thrashing her soul, as she sobs. Agnes needs to talk. She tells me about the final stages of Foluso's illness.

Thankfully, his father had been allowed to fly home, when it became clear that there wasn't much time left. The whole family was usually by Foluso's bedside and when the pain became unbearable, he would calmly ask them to please go home while he had some rest, not wanting them to see him suffer. The week before he died, Agnes, sensing the time was near, requested that he be discharged. Foluso suggested it be the following Monday. On that day, he quietly passed on. It was as if Faluso wanted to spare his family the physical details of his care.

This doesn't surprise me. Foluso had been an exceptional person, with a quiet wisdom and peace beyond his years. You had a sense that God was walking alongside him every step of the way. He was always more concerned about the needs of others than his own and endured the pain and humiliations of cancer without complaint. Agnes confided that one night, early on in his treatment, he had come into her room, knowing she wouldn't be asleep. He told her not to worry, he wasn't afraid of death. He also told her he loved her very much and she'd been a wonderful mother to him.

I'm aware that Agnes is needed and I've had more of her time than many others. She's swept away and James and I silently return to the car.

The beautiful May sunshine at the funeral feels wrong today, how dare we enjoy such light and hope when a young boy's body lies in darkness? It's a stark contrast to my mother's burial, when I was a teenager. At her graveside, the wind wailed and icy sleet stung exposed bits of skin; appropriate for the way I felt inside. I remember wearing my mother's new black shoes and thinking how grown up and pretty they were, hoping Mom would be pleased that I was looking marginally fashionable. We'd always battled over clothes and shoes. She was determined to buy me what she thought was the latest gear, where I only wanted conservative, blend-into-the-background things.

My grandmother had wanted an open casket at the funeral but, having been denied the opportunity to see my mother whilst she was still alive, I vehemently refused. I had only ever seen a dead body once before and that was an elderly uncle. He was like wax, creepy and nothing like the man I'd known. I didn't want that kind of memory of my mother. The last time I'd seen her she'd been the vibrant, caring Mom I loved. Despite dire warnings that I would regret it later in life (I haven't), my family respected my wishes.

I sobbed on the verge of hysteria throughout my mother's service but was deeply moved and comforted by the enormous turnout. People had to stand out in the street; there were so many mourners. There was solace in knowing that my mother had lived her life fully, with energy, joy and enthusiasm and had touched the lives of so many people. I hope Foluso's family will find comfort in the packed church this afternoon.

*

Over the months spent in the teenage cancer unit, we became friendly with several children and their families. Some of them seemed to be putting their lives back together and the Candlelighters' magazine featured reports on many who have survived childhood cancers of all sorts. But we also knew children who didn't make it.

We learned about a local teenager who had succumbed to four rare cancers around the time James was diagnosed. Her mother, with the support of her family, had set up the Laura Crane Trust to fund research into the rare cancers that affect people aged 15 to 25 years old. She had given up her full-time teaching career to devote herself to this cause, desperate that other families should not have to go through what they had. Cancers affecting this age group are often unusual and aggressive and the needs of the patients are different from those of either younger children or older adults.

We offered to help the charity and have spent a few hours standing in various supermarket collections. Then we decided to try the Three Peaks walk in the Yorkshire Dales to see if we could raise some more money. It's a 24-mile walk up and down three very tall peaks. We did it in ten hours and managed to collect just over £400 between us. Half of it went to the Parkinson's disease charity, which organised the walk, and the rest to the Laura Crane Trust.

We were amazed at the number of people doing the walk; there were buses full from all over. By the third peak, Howard's knees were agony and I wasn't much help, as I felt I had to run the last four to five miles. I couldn't *wait* to finish and had to do a different kind of movement other than walking. It was tough getting out of the car, at home, and we were worried what we'd be like the next day but, apart from a little stiffness, we were fine.

***

Our good friend, Tony, takes James to an airfield nearby and lets him drive his automatic car a few times before we're able to change ours and sort out a provisional licence. This is something grown-up, something James gets to do before any of his friends, something he really needs.

We trade in my car for a clutch-less Renault Clio. The technology is quite new for the cheaper, 'compact' end of the market. You still have to change gears, unlike an automatic transmission, but it's cheaper to buy and has better fuel consumption and performance. Apparently, it uses technology developed for Formula One racing cars, which pleases our son.

Tingling with anticipation, I hurry from work to collect my new purchase. I fill in all the last-minute paperwork, sign over my old vehicle and walk out to take possession of the new one. To my horror, it's the wrong car. I have ordered, paid for and need, five doors and this one only has three.

'What are you going to do?' the poor salesman asks. He looks awful, his colour has become a green shade of blanched milk and I can see a series of outcomes, each worse than the last, parade across his face.

'*What am I going to do?*' echoes in my mind. I have become so accustomed to unexpected blows; I don't even feel angry, just deflated. I suggest they give me a courtesy car and then I will collect the proper Clio in a week.

James is even more disappointed than I am, desperate as he is to drive 'his' new car. There is bewilderment and frustration in his angry words and the slamming sounds that follow him to his room. He clearly doesn't understand why the world seems to have turned against him.

A week later, I am sitting beside my son, peering between my scrunched-up lashes, fingers gripping the dash board and trying to breathe without screaming. Teaching ones' own precious child how to drive is one of life's more terrifying experiences. I am suddenly overwhelmed with a new appreciation and gratitude for my own father, who had so patiently helped me to practise my new skills decades earlier.

James loves driving and seems to learn quite easily. Our main concern is over-confidence and a tendency to lose concentration when chatting.

With his exams finished, James won't give much away, just tells us to expect the worst and hope for the best. Now, faced with nearly ten weeks holiday before beginning sixth-form college, we have divergent ideas of how he should spend his time. I think ironing, cooking and helping the rest of his working family, whereas he leans towards sleeping in, watching films and messing about with his friends. All of which is wonderfully normal. Getting a part-time job seems very problematical but eventually his previous employers at the newsagents take him on for a few hours a week in the shop.

*

In May 1976, the year after my first trip to England, I needed a summer job but didn't want to go home to live with my dad and stepmother. I found a position working as a nanny for a family in Boston who ran two children's summer camps. I was incredibly frugal but my dad was still horrified when he realised I was setting off for a city I'd never been to, 700 miles from home, to live with a family I'd never met, with only $3 (about £1.50) in my purse. Even in those days, it wasn't much money.

It was an interesting family. The father was Jewish and worked from home, during the winter, on the administration for the summer camps they owned. The mother had been a nun but since converted to Judaism and was studying at home for her PhD in psychology. The child was a little girl of four years old and I was her twelfth nanny, I think. Any time I told her she couldn't do something that I felt might be dangerous or inappropriate; she would run screaming to her parents. They would pet and cuddle her and make comments to the effect that I was in the wrong.

I was very grateful that the job would only be for two months, after which I would become a camp counsellor at one of their camps in Maine for eight weeks before returning to university. It was a wonderful time to be in Boston, as it was the US Bicentennial and I enjoyed using my days off to follow the Paul Revere trail and explore the historic city.

The summer camp was an experience. It was for Jewish girls, the boys' camp was nearby. The children were sent for eight weeks with a weekend in the middle for parents to visit, if they could or wanted to. I lived in a cabin with the six youngest girls, aged four to six. One of these was my former charge, the daughter of the owner, and one belonged to the other counsellor assigned to my cabin. Her husband worked in the boy's camp with their son and they saw this as a way of offering their children opportunities they might otherwise never have.

And it *was* a wonderful camp. It was huge, attractive and clean with log cabins and superb facilities, set in magnificent forests. I went with the little ones to their various activities throughout the day and supported them as ·they learned to swim, dance, act, sing, ride, trek in the hills, play tennis and a range of other games. But we also coped with the tears, nightmares and wet beds.

One day the owner's beautiful white Samoyed dog slipped into the fast flowing river and was weighed down by his heavy, wet fur. The banks were steep and, without thinking, I jumped in and pulled him out. I was bitten, had to go for a tetanus shot and was told off for my efforts but at least the dog was safe.

There was also a hurricane warning one night and the camp was evacuated to sleep in a local school. I volunteered, with a few others, to stay and look after the horses. We rushed about doing little bits of nothing, endlessly discussing the noises we could hear, pretending an assurance we didn't feel. I'm not sure what we would have done to help the horses had a hurricane actually hit, but nothing really happened apart from a very windy night.

My friend and university roommate, Kathy, was at the camp as well, but we were kept so busy we had little time for anything else. Being a year ahead of me she, and the other two girls that I had shared various accommodations with since beginning university, graduated that summer. In the autumn, I returned to my studies and shared an apartment with an anaesthetist called Ona. She worked shifts and led a full and very private life. I was kept busy working part-time and completing the courses needed to achieve my degree.

Through these busy years of learning, I continued to pray sporadically and read the Bible as well as other Christian books from time to time. Two books by Catherine Marshall stand out in my memory. In one, *To Live Again*, she talks about how she struggled to build a new life after the death of her beloved husband including insights, which I could relate to my own experiences, after the loss of my Mom.

In the other, *The Helper*, she described how the Holy Spirit worked in her life and could be that unexpected but persistent idea that seems to pop into your mind from nowhere to phone someone or do something you hadn't planned. She'd discovered over the years that it was always best to listen when it happened.

Her observation, that a day that didn't start with a prayer often felt unsatisfactory, seemed also to be mirrored in my life. I tried to be more disciplined because I longed for that quality that could be present when I invited God to join me in my day. The problem was that rigid discipline can result in formulaic, robotic prayer and He knows the difference. As with any relationship, it demanded time, energy and commitment.

My plan was to become a child psychologist, like my mother, but felt I would benefit from some life experience before attempting to help other people with their problems. I had majored in Social Sciences with a minor in psychology and a second minor in education, hoping that teaching would enable me to gain that experience and earn the money I would need to continue my studies. I had been accepted into a Master's Degree programme in Florida for the following autumn and only had my teaching practice to do before I could graduate.

Spotting an opportunity to do that placement in England, on an exchange course, I remembered the primary school I had visited there. It somehow seemed right. Later I would come to recognise that 'right' feeling as direction from God. Without hesitation, the girl who was once so ill from homesickness after just a night away from home, signed up for four months across an ocean.

***

It's not late but the boys have vanished to the bedroom end of the house. There's a book in my hand and the television is on but nothing much is going in. Something is niggling in the back of my mind.

Howard rubs his arm, again. I study him. Normally, he complains about repeated movements. The boys and I often diddle our feet and struggle to sit still and it drives him mad. What I see now shocks me. It's not just the bleached grey pallor of his skin or the shadowed hollows around his eyes. The strain that Howard's under at work, on top of our family situation, is taking a toll on his health. He isn't sleeping well but it's more than that. He's afraid.

'What's up with your arm?'

'Nothing, I'm just getting pins and needles.' He rubs it some more and suddenly becomes engrossed in the TV programme.

'You look awful. What's wrong?' I try to keep calm but firm. Howard hates the idea of being unwell.

'My chest hurts. It's hard to breathe.'

That's it. My mental calculator is computing probabilities and they all add up to terror.

'I'm phoning for an ambulance.' I leap out of my chair.

'No! It's not that bad.' His voice glitters like steel.

I can see that I'm making it worse. 'But pins and needles, chest pain, your family history... Howard, it could be a heart attack.' The panic is leaking out despite my best efforts.

'It's not a heart attack.'

'Well, I'm phoning the doctor, at least.'

'It's late.' His defence is weakening. I phone quickly and our brilliant GP arrives in minutes.

The doctor gives him a thorough check up and reassures us that Howard's heart is strong and his blood pressure fine.

'I think it's exhaustion from prolonged stress,' he tells us.

'We're sorry to have dragged you out for nothing,' Howard says.

'No, you did the right thing. Don't ever hesitate. If you think you might be having a heart attack, you ought to phone for an ambulance.'

I can hear the sincerity in the doctor's voice and see that he is relieved for us.

We decide to rest for a whole weekend. Like wearing children's armbands in an ocean storm, it helps a bit. So many emotions have been gripped tight for so long that relaxing, even for a couple of days, allows them to explode in my face. Bottomless pits of tears and flashes of anger erupt, as I prepare tea or queue at the supermarket.

*

In the early days of our marriage we had a lot to learn about each other. Howard and I were best friends as well as lovers and weren't afraid to argue when disagreements arose. Being the kind of person who likes to think out loud and bounce my ideas off someone else, to evaluate their feedback, I became extremely frustrated when Howard wouldn't play this game with me. I felt he wasn't prepared to consider my thoughts so would try to force him to comment.

One particular day, I'd pushed him too far and we had a huge row. He started packing a bag to leave me and just as quickly as he put things in, I threw them out, even hiding his keys. In the end he stomped out empty handed and walked all the way to the nearest town, some eight miles away. There he bought me a new kettle, turned and walked back.

Neither of us can remember what that quarrel was about but we did learn, from the experience, that we think differently. Howard *had* been listening to all that I had to say, thinking about it and giving me his carefully considered reply when it was ready, perhaps a few days later. Once I came to understand and respect that, I was less frustrated and we came to value this difference in our approach and saw how it strengthened us as a team.

Of course that didn't mean we never argued again. On another occasion that comes to mind, we were out walking and had a disagreement. I've no idea what it was about.

'Oh, for goodness sake, you're cutting your nose off to spite your face,' I yelled.

With a look of crackling fury, Howard turned and stormed off in front of me, striding out to put physical distance between us.

It was my turn to carry baby James in his pouch. This extra weight meant there was no way I could catch up or keep up with Howard. Feeling very hurt and angry, saying things we didn't really mean, I realised we'd backed ourselves into separate corners and were unable to reach out to one another.

In despair, I talked to God. I asked Him to take away my anger and help me to feel the love I had for Howard. Like cool salve on livid sunburn, peace spread within me.

With the intensity walked off and faced with a calm and loving wife, Howard's anger dissolved and whatever the problem had been, it was solved amicably.

***

The weekend of relaxation is all we can spare. I strap my emotions tightly back into their little box and get on with it.

James has another opportunity to train with the Para Olympic team. He's very disappointed, when he discovers that he missed the chance to be in Steven Spielberg's film *Saving Private Ryan*. Apparently, the team had been asked to appear as wounded soldiers.

The athletes teach James how to run and tell him about other teams which train to compete in badminton, basketball and other sports. He's more interested in these but still lacks the time and commitment needed to contend at that level.

David's birthday makes us pause. It's a year since James' diagnosis. David has a busy time with his paper round, rehearsals, then performing in a concert and three friends to sleep over on Saturday. The boys gorge themselves on mountains of unsuitable food they'd hidden in their bags, (and possibly smuggled drink) and one of the friends is sick in the night. Sunday, we have a family day together at the cinema, then more presents and a birthday tea at his grandma's on Monday. He is well and truly fifteen and very important to us, despite the fact our attention is so often focussed on his brother.

It's nearly the summer holidays before James finally gets his artificial leg. The muscles in his stump have all atrophied, making the socket loose.

The prosthesis is heavy, painful, cumbersome and generally hard work. It's especially difficult because, by this time, James is so quick and confident on his crutches and comfortable with his self-image.

Speaking to another man who lost his leg in an accident and went into prosthesis straight away, James tells us this chap was doing very well with his walking and already had a computerised knee but felt unable to go to the local swimming baths, as he couldn't face the reactions of others.

The new leg is more painful than it should be. It appears that the bone in James' stump is continuing to grow, threatening to burst through the skin. The doctors tell us he will need another operation, with two more weeks off school, just as he starts college. James is gutted. I suspect college offered the promise of a fresh start, where there would be people who didn't know about the cancer or the amputation. He could be 'normal', again.

*

An incident that happened the day before I was due to start high school flashes across my mind. The horse I rented had to live outside, as I couldn't afford the price of a stable. This often meant trudging across large open fields to catch her when I wanted a ride. There were some straggly apple trees in the field. I swung the bridle up to try to knock an apple down, to entice my mare, but the leather straps snagged on a branch. With a swift jerk on the reins, I managed to yank it free. Unfortunately, the metal bit smashed down into my face.

All my previous worry about what to wear, what to expect and how to make a good impression had been a waste of time. No one would notice any of that, not with a black eye and fat lip advertising for jokes and sniggers.

***

At last, the holiday is here. I could get weepy looking at Jim, with his crooked smile and dry sense of humour, and Rory, tall and athletic with Brad Pitt good looks. They've both made sacrifices and worked hard to save the money for their air fares to come on this trip with James. David easily fits in and the four of them roam the airport, too excited to sit down.

It's a long, long way to California but we have a three hour layover in Detroit. I let my family know and my brothers and their wives prepare a magnificent picnic and drive an hour to meet us. Unfortunately, the airport is massive and we never manage to find each other. I'm very disappointed and feel guilty for asking them to come on such a silly wild-goose chase.

Sitting all day is surprisingly exhausting and we've been awake for over twenty-four hours when we touch down in LA. The large, white people-carrier, with black tinted windows, that we hire, thrills the boys. They christen it the Mafia-mobile. We stop for supplies and, set loose in a supermarket, the lads run wild looking at the strange variety of foods lining the shelves. Fortunately, we're able to find our rented cottage without too many problems. At 1 am, we drop into our beds.

The beach is only a short walk from our accommodation and James manages fine with his crutches in the sand. The days blur past as we take the boys to Disneyland, Universal Studios, Six Flags Magic Mountain, Sea World, Tijuana, Mann's Chinese Theatre and do the Hollywood Stars' Homes Tour. They experience the longest, highest, scariest, newest rides in California. We also enjoy shopping, beach days and go to the cinema six times. In Sea World we see a rescued 'baby' grey whale being fed. In Triangle Square we drink iced smoothies on the roof and see space age fitments in the huge Nike store.

We develop catch phrases. 'I'm hungry,' brings a chorus of, 'let's have a Taco!' and peals of giddy laughter.

The boys are noisy, messy, bursting with energy and absolutely fantastic. My heart sings with pleasure to see them enjoy themselves after the time we've been through together. They all take a turn at sharing the cooking and that just adds to the memories. There's a blazing barbecue trying to cook very fatty hamburgers one night. Jim makes us all a Yorkshire fry up, aided by some 'beach babes' they'd collected that day. There was a heated debate about whether bacon should be cooked in a microwave or not. And Rory will never forget that pasta sheets come in two varieties, pre-cooked and not-precooked. Crunchy lasagne was a new one for us all.

I slip away in the early mornings. It's not so easy to shake off the stress of the past year and I still wake long before the others. The beach is empty, the sand cool with the night's damp. The air is crisp and clean blowing in off the grey waves and the rhythm of shushing sand is soothing. The sun will burn the clouds away in an hour but now I like the dull light, the white crash against black rock.

Our two weeks at the beach vanish into Time's purse. We pile everything into our Mafia-mobile and set off on the next leg of our adventure. This is even more exciting because we haven't booked any of it; we're just seeing where the whim, time and money will take us. We drive up the Pacific Coast Highway as far as Ventura, taking in tacky Venice Beach and lush Santa Monica along the way. The boys' conversations and observations ebb round me. I relax into semi-listening and watch the world go by.

In the late afternoon we cut inland, over the mountains to Bakersfield, where we find a cheap motel with a pool and stand-up breakfast in the lobby. We fill ourselves with enormous portions in a nearby Denny's restaurant then let the stiffness of travel wash away in the pool. It's twilight and too cold for me but the boys have to be chased from the water when their whoops and laughter disturbs other guests.

The next day, we drive across a flat, fertile valley with crops as far as you can see, before we reach the Sequoia National Park and climb another mountain range. The scenery is spectacularly breathtaking and the massive trees indescribable. The four nearly-full-grown, boys, Howard and I all link hands and still can't stretch around the trunk of one tree, even using James' crutches to extend our reach. The wonder of this place is slightly marred, for David in particular, by the handbook we're given at the entrance, which warns of the dangers of bears, cougars, ticks, snakes, *plague* and the water in the mountain streams.

The air in the park is liquid and green. The roads twist, climb and fall. We crane our necks to fill our eyes with all there is to see, hoping for a glimpse of a deer or a bear. Then suddenly, the car clears the forest and pauses on the lip of the mountain. Below us, in fierce sunlight, is the great bowl of Death Valley.

We edge down the side of the mountain. With each passing half hour the temperature soars. The colours surprise me but the heat is terrifying, when we stop and get out of the van. Reaching 120 degrees F in the shade, it burns the inside of my nose when I breathe and squeezes my chest tight. Howard revels in it and barely flits into the cool shop for a drink. How could anyone travel there without air-conditioning? I can't believe people once crossed this way in covered wagons.

It takes the rest of the day to drive across the desert, through the shimmering heat haze. The air is literally visible, belly dancing over the sand. We have to turn off the air conditioning. It's used so much extra fuel that we're in danger of running out. Mirages taunt us. I imagine myself walking to the nearest petrol station and start to pray. We coast up to the pumps on fumes.

As night drops, we rise and dip over small foothills. At the crest of one such rise, we see the 'over the top' opulence of Las Vegas spread before us. It's certainly best seen at night and has the most amazing, infectious electricity in the atmosphere. The hotels are each a full block in size, with shops, theatres, thousands of rooms, theme parks, live circuses, zoos and, of course, casinos. The power used for the lights alone would probably be enough to run a small country.

We're able to watch a performance of magicians, Penn and Teller, ride in a stretch limousine and visit a 'Wet and Wild' water park. It's still so hot, even in the shade, that I feel like I'm being blown dry by a giant hair dryer. James and Rory also claim to have been driven down the strip one evening, in a pink convertible, by two lovely girls.

After three nights, we head back to Newport Beach, calling in at the ghost town of Calico on the way. James and Rory can, and do, talk and debate about nothing, endlessly, mile after mile. In exasperation, Jim challenges them to be silent for half and hour. I doubt it will be possible but they take it with their usual competitive spirit and tension flows from the car. Our last day is spent body surfing, swimming and sunbathing; squeezing in one more film before we head to the airport.

*

We fly together as far as Detroit, when we have to say goodbye to Howard, Jim and Rory. They are returning to the UK, whilst my boys and I continue on to Baltimore for an action-packed visit with my aunt, uncle and cousins there. We see Washington DC from a Tour-bus, visit the Air and Space Museum, have a picnic on the Potomac and spend precious time with these dear relatives who've shared our worries.

Last, but certainly not least, we return to Michigan and Dad, Lynda, my step-sister, brothers and their families. They are delighted and amazed at how well James looks and how tall David is, now over 6 foot.

'I was bracing myself for the worst,' Keith confides to me, as we watch our children play in the pool. 'I'm so surprised and relieved.' He turns away. His eyes are moist.

The little girls, Karly aged 3 and Kelsey aged 4, are the most interesting. They spend some time with James when we first arrive then come to find me and demand to know when he is going to get his leg back and how it had been 'broken'. It's quite tricky answering such big questions without frightening them. Having managed to their satisfaction, they then want to know if I am old and why I have little hairs around my mouth. Kelsey tells me her mom is never going to get old.

Ready to rejoin the boys, Kelsey wants to know if James can remember when he was 'lower' (younger?). We wonder if she can remember him from our previous visit eighteen months earlier. Watching him doing back flips and somersaults off the diving board, she turns to me and says, in hushed tones, "Isn't he talented!"

The children adore their 'big' cousins just as they are. Kevin invites one of his friends in to meet them and proceeds to tell the boy that James has had cancer and only has one leg. His mother is mortified but this is honest and open. We are more used to it, I guess.

During the week that we are visiting with my family, we have several phone calls from Howard to see how we're going on. There is something wrong, I can hear it in his voice, but he keeps assuring me all is well, he's just missing us.

Chapter 6

After a long flight through the night, my muscles relax at the sight of Howard waiting for us at the airport. The visit to my family had been very important for us all but I missed my husband and am glad to be home. It's a relief to hand over the burden of luggage and boys, as he leads us out to his new company Audi. Cars are a passion with Howard and I'm surprised that he isn't more excited about it but too weary to give it much thought. On the way home, memories pop to the surface of our journey-fuddled minds. Conversation is disjointed and sporadic. Howard's questions and responses seem forced, as if he's angry about something.

Once we're safely inside, Howard sits us down and shares the terrible secret he's carried for the past week.

'Louise is dead.'

I can't breathe. I can't take it in. I'm angry. It must be a joke, but I can see from Howard's face that it isn't. I want to scream or run away or fight to get her back. Words don't make sense. I go and stand in the shower and the tears come. I'm afraid they won't stop.

'When we got back, jet-lagged and weary,' Howard sits beside me on the bed and relives his nightmare, 'I dropped Jim and Rory off and called in at the supermarket for a few essentials.'

'I ran into Uncle Lesley in the car park and he started telling me how sorry he was.' It was a cruel place to learn that his beautiful sister had been knocked down and killed on a pedestrian crossing a few days earlier.

'He didn't realise that I didn't know.'

A teenage boy, possibly under the influence of something, had been driving three times the speed limit round a blind corner, through a village, and not seen her in time. Louise was with her husband and friends enjoying a pleasant evening one moment and gone the next. Similar to my mother and cousin, she'd been 36 years old and touched many lives with joy. The mourners filled the building and spilled out into the street.

Having missed the funeral myself, it still doesn't seem real. I go to see Peter, Louise's husband. He looks hollow, shocked and utterly devastated yet concerned for others, trying to make us smile with his memories. We visit Mum, so distressed by the months of trauma we've been through with her grandson. She looks squeezed out, every footstep an effort. She hasn't even the strength to cry.

*

Louise, I see her in my mind, always with a different hairstyle, full of sparkle and fun. She was especially good at choosing gifts for people, thoughtful and forgiving. Her sleeves would be pushed up and she'd be stuck in before a word was spoken, if there was help needed. She loved to pop in for a visit when the *Coronation Street* soap opera came on so she could tease us for watching it. Howard would pretend to be furious and lock her out. Throughout the valleys around Huddersfield, her beautiful singing voice was well known.

Her father hadn't approved of her choice of Peter but she'd married him anyway. Cynthia also defied Geoffrey to attend her daughter's quiet wedding. Geoffrey had been frightened that Peter was too old for Louise. Much older, divorced and with children already, Peter had made it clear he didn't want any more. We worried that Louise would be alone, if he died before her, as seemed likely. But she was headstrong and she loved him.

Peter's gift for seeing the humour in people and situations would be sorely tested now.

***

Two days later, it's results day. James allows me to drive him to school but I'm forbidden to get out of the car. These grades are so important for James' self esteem, to enable him to reclaim his life. He has the door open before I'm fully stopped.

'See ya later, Mum,' he calls over his shoulder.

'I'll wait here, shall I? You will come out and let me know how you've done, won't you?'

'Why do you need to know?' He's dancing on the spot, full of fear and excitement. He doesn't want the extra pressure of these results being important to anyone else.

'Because I care about you!' I try not to shout this at him. The ego-centricity of teenagers is staggering but I know I was probably the same. I flash back to the moment James told me I could no longer walk him to school, when he moved up to the juniors at seven years old. I know I shouldn't hold on so tight but it's very hard to let go.

He's earned an incredible 6 As, 3 A*s and a B in physics. James goes off to celebrate with his friends and I collapse from nervous exhaustion after sharing the news with everyone I know.

There is no rest, though. The next day James and I sit slumped side by side in the waiting room of Paediatric Oncology. We've already been for the x-rays; we just need the results – results that are infinitely more important than those we got yesterday. I scrutinise my son for signs of disease. He looks awful but then so do I. Slammed by grief after the high of our holiday, lifted by James' achievement, afraid of what the doctor might say, I wonder how much more my system can take.

It's good news, another month's respite. There's room in my brain now for all the errands we must run before school starts again next week. We pause for lunch out to celebrate.

'Where have you been?' David screams at us, when we walk in the house.

I've never seen him so wild. We'd phoned Howard with the good news, from the hospital but never thought about David. He'd worked himself up into a panic because we were so long, convinced the cancer had come back. Louise's sudden death had made such a possibility so much more real to him. I'm ashamed of my own ego-centricity now.

Two days later, I drop the boys off at Scammonden reservoir. It's early, about 8 am. They will be learning to sail with the scouts. The sun is shining and the day stretches before me, my mind already filling with things I have to do. I switch the radio on and listen in disbelief. The news is full of the death of Princess Diana.

I have to pull over. I can't breathe and tears are blurring my vision. She's the same age as Louise and all the loss I feel for my dear sister-in-law roars to the surface. William is the same age as I was when I lost my mother. I pray for Diana's children.

*

Watching the royal family struggle to find the right response to the Princess' death, I was reminded of the impact a failed marriage can have on the wider family.

Just as my brother Keith prepared for his wedding to Monique, the marriage between my dad and Nicki came to an end. I had been shocked when I received a letter informing me of their impending divorce, even though I knew they'd been unhappy for years. Somehow a divorce reverberates through other marriages, threatening the trust they're based on. I'd written to them both imploring them to be sure, to seek help, but to no avail. Nicki joined Alcoholics Anonymous but it was too late and for the wrong reasons. There was too much pain and scar tissue between them.

Despite their personal troubles they both tried extremely hard to put aside their animosity for the sake of my brother's wedding. My dad, after years of suppressed grief and stress, had developed a medical condition which affected his ability to swallow. At times of particular stress, it would flare up. His total inability to eat anything and subsequent weight loss were the only obvious signs of his distress.

We stayed with Nicki in my parent's house. My dad had moved out to a small apartment, but we spent as much time as we could with him. It was a very snowy February and we enjoyed skiing, snowmobiling, sledging, tobogganing and even a horse-drawn wagon ride. This was in addition to the parties, rehearsal dinner and other family celebrations. Aunts, uncles, cousins and grandparents came from all over to share in the joy. The wedding was held on Valentine's Day and was lovely.

As an extra treat my dad paid for us to have a night at the Inn on the Park hotel in Toronto, before we flew home. This was the hotel we'd had our honeymoon in and it was fun, if a little strange, to be back there with our children. Nicki had driven us to Toronto and enjoyed taking in the sights with us.

In June, my dad came over to England. Among other things, we took him hiking in the Lake District. The exercise and scenery worked their healing power. He was totally exhausted and it was reassuring to watch him unwind and begin to rebuild his health. He was so tired; he actually fell asleep in the middle of David's fourth birthday party, surrounded by boisterous four- and five-year-old children.

We had lunch together; just the two of us, and Dad shared some of the trauma he'd been through with Nicki. She'd written me lengthy letters and had given us her side of things whilst we'd been over for the wedding. It was clear there would be no reconciliation.

My dad visited several times over the subsequent years, more frequently than usual and I was glad that he found our home to be a place of rest and retreat. He was just as sociable as ever though, which was brought home to us by an experience in the local pub. Saddled with young children, as we were, we seldom managed to go ourselves. But we went in with my dad and were floored when the bartender greeted him like a long lost friend and knew him by name.

***

It's a precious weekend and Howard and I are alone in the living room. We haven't the energy to put the television on. The white noise in my brain is deafening and my body feels as if it's being buffeted by an icy wind. Lying on the settee, Howard's eyes are open and unfocussed.

'We can't go on like this.' I look at Howard and see deep creases worn into his face. Our trip to California had been a lifesaver for him. He certainly couldn't have borne the tragedy of his sister's death in the state he'd been in before we'd gone.

He says nothing. I can see the muscle in his jaw clench. The time is fast approaching when he will have to begin to live away for part of each week.

'You hate this crisis management, every step forward spoiled by bullyboy tactics.' I've listened for months to Howard's stories of fighting fires for the people below him and forever trying to appease those above.

'What choice do we have?' His tone is sharp. I can hear a flash of anger in the defeat. 'I understand why you and the boys can't move to Stratford but I don't see what else I can do.'

'Sweetheart, the pressure you're under is punishing. The broken promises and the perpetual exhaustion are too much.' I can feel she-bear defensiveness kick in.

This is not an earth shattering revelation. There is no response.

'You don't have anything left to enjoy your life.' I'm up and pacing around the room, ready to fight the world to protect my family. 'It's not worth the damage to your health.' Whilst he's sleeping a bit better, he's still struggling with his stomach and the doctor's having trouble getting to the bottom of the problem.

I take a breath. 'You should quit this job.'

'But how will we manage?' My husband is nothing if not realistic.

'You'll find another job. I'm back at work now. If James needs us, you can look after him.' The words are rushing out. 'We've always managed to live happily, whether we've had any money or not.'

'Your wage alone won't pay the mortgage,' he says, quietly.

'We could sell this house and buy something much smaller, if we have to.' I stoop and put my arms around him. 'I'd rather live in a cardboard box than watch you die this slow death.' His shoulders drop and he feels heavy in my arms.

In the morning, Howard hands in his letter of resignation.

His bosses aren't surprised, when Howard tells them he wants to leave. They offer him a choice between a lesser job, nearer home or a redundancy package but make us wait for the details. It's a huge relief to have made the decision but there's yet another layer of anxiety, as we face an 'unknown' future. For a compulsive planner like me, it's the ultimate in scariness and

I've had a lot of it lately. Logically, we never know what tomorrow will bring and we only fool ourselves with the false security blanket of our plans. I know 'faith' is the answer but it's easier said than done, sometimes. I have no regrets about this decision we've made, though. If it's a choice between trusting God and chasing money, I'll go with God every time.

*

When it became clear to my dad that I was really going to marry my Englishman, he tried very hard to persuade us to live in America. He offered Howard a job at a fabulous wage and reminded me that I'd been accepted to do my master's degree. I would be able to earn considerably more money as a psychologist than as a teacher, especially in the US.

But the stories of drug abuse and promiscuity in my high school, the statistics for crime and broken marriages convinced us that Britain was probably a better place to raise children. We liked the idea of belonging in a community where generations of Howard's family had lived. And I loved teaching. It wasn't at all difficult to put our future family and job satisfaction before money. The hard part, for me, was being so far from my relatives. But even if I'd gone to Florida to study, I'd still have had a long-distance relationship with my own family.

Then years later, when our boys were small and Howard was offered a job after three months on the dole, we never considered turning it down – despite the fact that we would be bringing in less money than we were getting in benefits. To us it was a chance for Howard to prove himself, to work his way up, make his own possibilities. And we've never been sorry about these choices, either.

***

Ready or not, 'Life' gets back into top gear. David blossoms at school, now that he's in the class of oldest pupils and his brother's left. He enjoys a sailing course and a full day at the Young Film Makers Festival. With his saxophone, he takes part in an open-air Jazz Festival as well as many other concerts and his Big Band wins through to perform at the Royal Albert Hall in London for the Proms. But it's mid-week.

This is so hard. I'm desperate to get my life back on track, to prove I can cope. There is the OFSTED inspection looming so pressure at school is manic. I daren't ask for any more time off. Howard is caught in limbo and likewise doesn't feel he can skip off to London. To our shame, we allow ourselves to be blinded to the importance of this event for our undemanding son and consol ourselves that at least his grandparents and uncle are there to support him. This is a decision I do regret.

James settles quickly into the sixth-form college. Much like university, the students are not expected to be in class all the time, only about eighteen hours a week, leaving lots of free time to go into town, meet with friends, study, etc. There are occasional collisions of opinion between parents and child, over best use of time, but on the whole both sides make the adjustment.

Two incidents, right at the beginning, pose a challenge. Wearing his artificial leg, it isn't obvious that James is an amputee. With some discomfort he tells me about one teacher's jokey off-hand comments about one-legged people. I want to storm into the college and smack this so-called professional but realise James will have to learn to deal with this kind of ignorance in his own way. Then in his first debate lesson, the class are asked to compare Princess Diana's death to that of a local woman – his Auntie Louise.

We are also in a conflict surrounding the surgery James needs on his stump. The specialist tells us James ought to do more exercise to build up the muscles before the operation can go ahead. James tries to comply and is wearing his leg every day, despite the pain but each time we return to the hospital we are told it isn't enough. This happens several times. His physiotherapist and the one from the Para Olympic team both strongly disagree and feel the operation should be done as soon as possible.

We go to our GP and ask whether he thinks the specialist is delaying the surgery more out of a lack of beds then for clinical reasons. When we remind him that we have private medical insurance, the operation is booked within a few days. I wonder how many people continue to suffer because they are poor.

James spends his seventeenth birthday in hospital having a re-amputation. There is another more medical term for it but this is how I understand it. The operation goes well but it still means a lot more pain for my stoical son to bear. Another prosthesis will have to be made and the stump will have to heal, so many more weeks without an artificial leg.

It also means another first day for James, at college this time, without a leg. I long to help, to protect him from the startled expressions, the other people who don't know what to say or think or do, but realise it's impossible. In the event, he lifts his chin, puts on his cheekiest grin and gets on with it, as usual.

*

There are lots of first days scattered through life. Education was only my minor subject at university and, up to my arrival in Barnsley, I had only limited and specific contact with children. For example, teaching a PE or drama lesson in a local school one afternoon a week for 10 weeks or so. In my psychology courses, I'd been a teaching assistant, in charge of my own group of university students, for a term, and had also worked with a nursery child who didn't know how to play with other children. As to how they taught children in England, I only had that one visit to a school in Oxford, two years previously. We did have some lectures and time for preparation at the college before we began our placements but I still felt woefully inadequate.

The first day of my seven-week teaching practice arrived and I felt naked. Surely, everyone would be able to see that I was a fraud and didn't know what I was doing. As I walked in, a thin, pale woman hurried up to me.

'You're to be in my class.' She led me to the empty room and stood twisting her hands together. She wouldn't look at me.

'I've only just returned, you see.' Her words clattered at speed. 'Nervous breakdown,' her voice dropped. 'I'll be using the time that you're here to overhaul the school's library.' Then she was gone.

I looked around and didn't know where to start. Within what seemed like moments, children began to arrive and the day took hold. I felt as if I was gripping onto a spinning round-a-bout and could only let go and tumble in the grass when the last child left.

It was a vertically streamed infant class of children from 4 to 7 years old and I loved it. I had the freedom to make mistakes and was forced to evaluate my own performance and solve the problems that came along. It was incredibly intense, as I learned how to plan, prepare resources, create ·displays and all the myriad skills needed to teach.

The college sent tutors who observed me and offered 'crits' (written comments/criticisms about your teaching), which were new to me. At first I found them painful and took them personally but soon began to see how they could help me. Almost before I knew it, the seven week teaching practice was finished and so was my time at the college.

Just as a little postscript to this: nearly thirty years later I met someone who had been a child in that class and who remembered me as the person who had sparked his lifelong interest in bats. Despite the difficulties, teaching is a hugely responsible and immeasurably rewarding profession.

***

Our decision to put life first pays off. Howard's company offers him the opportunity to write his own job description, working much nearer to home, at the same salary, for a three-month trial period. He can then choose to stay in the new job or take the redundancy package. This lifts some of the pressure off and the company's eagerness to keep him boosts Howard's self-confidence. He will continue to be needed in Stratford until December, when they hope a replacement will be in place. But this is easier to bear with an end in sight.

Despite the promised improvements at work (they fire Howard's replacement after a very short time) he continues to suffer from chest pains and begins to experience 'pins and needles' in his arms and discomfort in his shoulder. After several possibilities are unsuccessfully explored, he is sent for an MRI to eliminate the likelihood of a tumour pressing on a nerve in his neck.

'The first thing they asked was if I'd ever had any metal in my eyes before,' Howard tells me, when he gets home. 'It seemed a strange question. I mentioned the fragments from that tyre fitting job, sixteen years ago. I told them I'd had my eyeball scraped at the hospital but they still sent me for an X-ray first. The technician explained that the MRI is a magnetic imaging machine, which uses extremely powerful magnets. If even the tiniest fragment of metal had worked its way into my eye or brain, it would instantly be pulled straight out.'

I can visualise this and feel queasy.

'Then they squeezed me into a tight metal tube and told me to keep absolutely still. I wasn't even allowed to swallow at one point.' Howard is warming to his story, now the experience is behind him. 'The machine thundered, like a team of jackhammers, next to my ears. You've never heard anything like it. At one point a little tear dribbled out of the corner of my eye and I started to think it was a drop of blood.'

I wonder where such bravery comes from. I can only imagine myself screaming in panic.

'When it was finally over, after what seemed like an hour, I walked back out to reception and noticed a huge jar full of earplugs on the receptionist's desk. When I questioned why I hadn't been offered any, the dozy woman just looked at me and said, "you didn't ask."'

It takes weeks and several phone calls to obtain the results of these tests. The suspicion of cancer sits like a stinking corpse in the corner of our life and we try to pretend it isn't there. Finally, Howard is told that it isn't a tumour. The problem is most likely a form of arthritis. If the calcification continues to develop in the joints, pressing on the spinal cord, he will probably need surgery, with a very big risk of paralysis.

The thought of this forces Howard to be more realistic in the work he's willing to accept and he becomes healthier, happier and more effective as a result. With physiotherapy and a new special orthopaedic pillow, his symptoms begin to ease. The company are again reminded of Howard's value to them when he's able to rush to the rescue after another key man collapses in his home from burst polyps in his intestines.

*

Whatever his value is to the company, I can't imagine my life without Howard but it could have been very different. When my friend and I were going for badminton lessons, all those years ago, I had a strange experience. Perhaps because of that dowdy feeling you get after your body has expanded and contracted by two stone or more, the incessant demands of a hungry baby and boisterous toddler, the general sublimation of self, there is vulnerability in new motherhood.

At the sports centre, I noticed a man noticing me and I was flattered. For a moment I felt like a thirteen-year-old. I wondered if he would be there next week and notice me again. Then I stopped. What was I thinking? I had the most wonderful husband and two precious children. I prayed that these unbidden thoughts and the temptation to my vanity could be removed. Instantly, all thought or interest permanently vanished, replaced by a glorious feeling of joy and appreciation of the blessings I already had. I wouldn't be able to describe or even recognise this other person again if I saw him, neither has anything like that happened since.

***

Having Howard around more is proving very important, as the OFSTED inspection draws ever closer and the pressure at school increases. It's been building for twelve months and it feels like we're trying to create a life-sized Angel of the North out of sand. Large chunks of every 'holiday' have been spent planning, preparing labels and resources, cleaning and painting. In an effort to prepare us, the headteacher has called in a series of 'experts' to observe and advise. They all criticise us for different things and give conflicting advice, resulting in a frenzy of activity, self-doubt and exhaustion.

One afternoon, I've waved off the last child and am busy tidying my classroom. I'm relieved that the expert of the day, Ms Q, hasn't had time to watch me teach. Almost as soon as this thought has drifted across my mind, she appears.

'Hello.' I push my face into what I hope is a welcoming smile.

Nothing.

'My planning is here.' I move to the table I use as a base and square up the file with my plans neatly displayed.

She makes no move in my direction, just walks a rapid circuit of the room and leaves.

I finish my fettling, pile work into my bag and make my way through the school to the front door. There is a small crowd of colleagues gathered round the headteacher. The expert has left the building, time to castigate ourselves with her comments. As I approach, one of the teachers turns in my direction. Her face looks drained. In hushed tones, she tells me the woman has reduced another teacher to tears.

The headteacher looks up at me. 'On her way out of the school, Ms Q said, "That Canadian teacher's planning is inappropriate." I assume she meant you.'

'And how would she know this?' I ask. I can feel fury bubbling in my guts. 'She whizzed round my classroom without a word to me or a glance at my planning and the children had already left.'

But the headteacher isn't interested. She's moving away busily planning what further changes we can make in the days before OFSTED arrive.

'Did she have any suggestions as to how "my planning" could be improved or in what way it was inappropriate?' But I am asking myself, the others have scurried away.

I can't imagine what benefit there could be for the children to have their teachers running round like rodents in a wheel creating nothing but smoke and tears. Each day seems to bring a new drama. No one is sleeping or smiling. Howard listens to my reports then tries to remind me that our school is just a little goldfish bowl in the ocean of life. James' cancer checks also help me to keep this whole process in some kind of perspective.

When the inspection finally arrives, I'm disappointed that it isn't a more constructive and positive experience. My headteacher, apparently, asked them to give me some space, given my circumstances, so many of the inspectors seem reluctant to speak to me. It's very kind of them all but it increases my feeling of being a victim by not having a voice in the proceedings.

It's very disconcerting to have someone watch you, making copious notes, then not provide you with any feedback. My lessons are all deemed to be fine but it would have been helpful to have the opportunity to discuss why I had been doing what I was doing and to be given some suggestions for ways in which I could improve.

I do have one funny moment during the week-long inspection. My music lesson seems to be going along so well that I'm almost able to forget the suited, silent man in the corner. The children listen carefully to guess which instruments are being played behind a screen and their concentration is palpable, as they try to repeat musical patterns created by other children. But the smile freezes on my face, when I suddenly realise I've come to the end of my planning and there are still five minutes until home time. My mind goes completely blank. I can't remember a single song to sing with the children. My eyes scan the room for inspiration and light on the inspector.

'You must see some wonderful music lessons on your travels round the country. I wonder if you have a favourite song you'd like to teach us?' A small voice in my head is screaming at me and questioning my sanity.

The inspector looks stunned for a moment then gathers his wits and smiles. He teaches us a silly version of 'Ten in a Bed' that I've never heard before, with funny actions, and the children love it. They respond with gusto and leave in giggles. Even the inspector looks as though he's enjoyed himself.

*

It reminds me of another fear-facing event that happened one morning a few years earlier. Before the children came in, a very sizeable mother, swollen with anger, blazed into my classroom screaming words and spittle in my face.

'My daughter is *not* to bring a library book home *ever* again! My toddler might *wreck* the book and I *won't* be able to pay for it.'

In a calm, quiet voice, I managed to say, 'That's not a problem at all. I understand your difficulty. Would it be all right if your little girl chooses a book with the other children and keeps it in her drawer at school? Perhaps you could share it with her in the mornings, when you bring her in?'

The response was instant and dramatic. It was as if I'd punctured her with a tiny pin; she deflated and was left almost speechless. She had obviously had to work herself up to such a pitch just to speak to a teacher. I couldn't help wondering what her previous experiences of school had been. When I complimented her on her unusual purple shoes, I had a friend for life and she even began to come into school to help, not long after that.

Teaching, especially young children, is so much more then the lessons you plan and the way you deliver them. Building partnerships with parents is a big part of the job. Is there such a thing as the perfect human parent? I doubt it. What would be right for one child, wouldn't work for another. As a teacher, I saw all sorts of parents.

Some of the most forlorn children are the ones whose mothers want to do everything for them. I once taught a child, nearly five years old, who mutely held out his coat, hat and mittens to me at the first playtime.

"What would you like, Luvvy?" I asked, gently.

"Coat" was the timid reply.

"What would you like me to do with your coat?" I coaxed. He didn't even know how to ask for help. When I suggested he try to put it on himself and I would help if he got stuck, he was mortified. Of course, he wasn't able to dress himself for PE either. Once he'd mastered these basic skills, and it took time, I had him demonstrate in the sharing assembly in front of the rest of the school and we all celebrated his achievement.

At the same time, I had to carefully help the mother to see that every time you do something for your child, your actions tell him/her that you don't think they're capable of doing it for themselves. The harder, but more loving, response is to patiently encourage and praise attempts at independence, allowing them to try a little bit more than even they think they can do. Sadly,

I've known children starting school who didn't know how to use a knife and fork, a toilet or even one child who could barely walk, having been carried everywhere. These children stand out from their peers and often then have trouble making friends.

***

On Remembrance Sunday, a charity concert is held in Louise's memory. Two of the choirs, that she'd been involved with, perform. Matthew, Simeon and his wife, Erica, come up from London for the event. Listening to words celebrating Louise's life and immersed in the music that she loved, I can almost feel her sitting beside me at times. In my mind, I see again Lorraine and Louise dressed in black leotards, whiskers painted on their cheeks, singing the cat's duet or feel tears build with the haunting music from Handel's *Messiah*.

Sadly, Simeon's car is broken into whilst we're in the concert hall. Nothing appears to have been stolen but there's glass all over the back seat. It's been a very busy night for vandals, apparently, so he isn't able to have it repaired until the next day. It means a day's work missed for both Simeon and Matthew.

James passes his driving test, first time, and promptly goes out and has a small bump in my car. He'd got caught up in a one-way system in a car park and wasn't sure what to do. As he was trying to carefully reverse, an impatient taxi driver tried to push past and caught his bumper from behind. We know this version of events is accurate because the police just happened to be there at the time. We arrange six 'Pass Plus' lessons to give him more experience, as well as instruction in motorway and night driving.

Both boys prepare to undertake the final requirements for the Queen Scout Award, the highest award in scouting. My dad had achieved the equivalent, Eagle Scout, and they knew he would be very proud if they could do the same. David does his community service helping in my school and James, who helped out in a geriatric ward one day a week last year, switches to a psychiatric unit.

Howard and I attend an annual dinner dance, in aid of the Laura Crane Teenage Cancer Trust. Through mutual friends, we are acquainted with Laura's mum, Jacqui, and she knows some of James' story. We're with friends and the evening is full of laughter, fund raising activities, dancing and good food. There are speeches about the work of the trust and a brief history of Laura, her life and the cancers that ended it too soon.

Escaping to the Ladies room, the sudden quiet emphasises the noise-induced humming in my ears. I open the door and Jacqui turns from the hand drier. We're alone, surrounded by mirrors. She looks at me, with all the misery of loss in her face.

'Why has James survived, when Laura didn't?' she asks me.

My breath catches. There is no answer to give. I hope my eyes show how my heart breaks for her. Her daughter had been kind and loving, generously volunteering at the local hospice. She didn't deserve to die any more than any of the other children we've met. *Where's God in this?*

*

We have bare breeze-block walls and clear glass in the windows of our chapel, in keeping with Methodist simplicity. I often sit by the slim arched windows and look out over the small garden whilst listening to the sermons. Beyond the grass of the church lawn, the river has carved a deep dip for itself. On the other bank is a footpath, through the trees, connecting the car park with the main part of the small town. I like to watch people going about their business in the world outside the church.

Lay preachers are used regularly in the Methodist tradition. These are ordinary people, with other jobs, who've taken some training and lead worship on a voluntary basis. It helps to spread the paid preachers further and allows the congregations to experience a wide range of viewpoints and approaches.

One Sunday in spring, warm tears wet my cheeks, as I watched two little girls skip along the path beyond the river. Dappled sunlight splashed their bright heads. I remembered that lightness of childhood, when my body was too full of life to merely walk.

Simon was 'preaching' and his promising words were read to us by an assistant. Simon has quite severe cerebral palsy. He painstakingly prepares his services using a specially adapted computer, because he can't speak, but he was there, facing us at the front of the church. Strapped in his wheelchair, his white-gloved fingers danced and his face was alive with pleasure. His sermon was peppered with humour and he sometimes struggled not to laugh before the punch lines he knew were coming.

Simon will never know what most of us take for granted. Experiences like the sheer pleasure there is in skipping. But my tears were not for Simon. They were for all the children and adults who will never know the joy and freedom Simon has found in his faith. *or this*

***

Walking across the quiet car park behind my church, I'm thinking about the things I need to do in the village.

'Good morning, Kimm. How're things?'

I look up and smile to see Brian and Betty coming towards me. Rumpled with years they are nevertheless a couple of the granite foundation stones of our community. They've known Howard since he was a boy and Betty ran the mobile baby clinic that James attended for the first few years of his life. Brian is one of the lay preachers in our church. Both doctors, they remind me of my aunt and uncle and have always been generous with their precious time, asking about James and listening to my long tales about his progress.

'We're in the second year since his treatment finished.' I can see my pleasure in this landmark reflected in their faces. 'He only has to go for check-ups every other month, now.'

'That is good news.' Betty pats me on the shoulder.

'The doctors are happy to try to fit the check-ups into school holidays as often as they can so James won't miss too much time at college.' This flexibility allows the knot in my core to relax a fraction. 'They've done a load of tests this time and taken blood, which they haven't done before.' I pause to study their reaction to this, to gauge if I should be worried. Their expressions remain open and unsurprised.

'They tell me it's to determine if there's been any long-term damage done to his organs from the chemotherapy.'

'That's normal procedure,' Brian says.

The knot loosens a little more. I love the word "normal".

'Your faith has been a real inspiration to us, Kimm.'

My breath snags and tears blur my eyes. I can't believe that God can use even me, as poor a Christian as I often feel I am, to reach out to other people, especially people who are so much further along the path towards knowing Him.

*

In the waiting room, we learn that two other children, diagnosed at the same time as James, are back in treatment with secondary cancers and a third died suddenly after appearing to do well. Frozen bricks weigh heavy in my guts and I say a swift, silent prayer for them and their families.

I'm instantly on alert, when it's our turn to go in and Dr Edwards greets us. He's the 'big cheese' in paediatric oncology and I'm afraid he must be here because it's bad news.

He's friendly and chirpy. He and James share stories, while we settle into our chairs.

'Now, about your results,' he shuffles the papers in front of him, 'they look good.'

My relief is so explosive I can hardly hear what else the doctor has to say.

'The blood and heart tests indicate there hasn't been any permanent damage as a result of the treatment. I think there's little risk now of the cancer returning. It was so aggressive that if it were going to reappear, it would have done so by now.'

I want to kiss this man. I want to sing and shout and fly. We had begun to hope as much but to hear it from this expert gives wings to my joy. I practically run from the room to phone Howard.

Next to this news, the fact that James is still struggling to use an artificial leg regularly seems less important. After two 'emergency' appointments, for open sores, at the limb-fitting hospital, they decide to make him another new leg and the saga wears on. At least he's developed quite remarkable arm and shoulder muscles, with which to impress the girls, from all the crutching he's done.

*

The punishing rhythm of anxiety and relief is diluted by half, now that James' ·check-ups are less frequent. Tentatively, we ease back into more ordinary life.

We take David and a couple of his friends to Oasis Holiday Park for a long weekend, to celebrate his sixteenth birthday. James brings a friend along, as well, and they all have a fantastic time. We hardly see them, apart from when they swarm in and strip the fridge and cupboards of food and drink, leaving wet towels and sweaty socks in their wake. The freedom and activities available are perfect for active teenagers. Howard and I collapse in a little heap and wonder where their childhoods have gone. I can't help but reflect on the two years since David's fourteenth birthday.

With OFSTED behind us, I resume my management role and add ICT coordinator to my other responsibilities. Luckily, I have David at home to help me master new computer skills and software before I have to show the other staff what to do. He huffs with exasperation and demonstrates with blur-fast fingers. I have to beg his patience to talk me through, as I fumblingly attempt to follow his instructions.

We all try to recover our equilibrium at school. The build-up was so stressful and of such duration that we're left feeling deflated. Everyone moves more slowly. Laughter and motivation are muffled by a blanket of apathy. Now there's an 'action plan', as a result of our inspection, and a steady stream of new initiatives but it's difficult to generate much enthusiasm

'James, there's a letter for you.' I hold the envelope out to my son who's scrounging in the fridge. 'Tea will be ready soon. Don't eat too much.' I go back to the food preparation.

'What is this?' James frowns over the contents of the letter in his hand. He reads it through again then drops it on the kitchen counter and heads for his bedroom.

Scanning the page, I feel a little shiver of equal parts pride and concern. I follow James. He won't look at me.

'What's the problem?' I ask.

'They want to give me the Chief Scout's Meritorious Conduct Medal, Mum, for bravery.' He grimaces at me. 'I haven't done anything brave. I haven't done anything anyone else wouldn't have done.'

'But you have been brave, James,' I say, gently. I long to rest my hand on his shoulder but this son doesn't like to be touched. 'You didn't hide away. When you were ill, you still struggled into school, as often as you possibly could. You were brave enough to have the amputation and didn't give up just because you lost your leg. What about the thirty-mile walk you guys did this summer?'

That raises a small smile. James, David and three of their friends had planned, organised and undertaken the walk as part of their Queen Scout challenge. One of the lads wasn't in the scouts but wanted to go along. They had great fun staging all their photos with this boy appearing in different guises in the background on every one; a sort of 'Where's Daniel?' instead of 'Where's Wally?'

'But they want to do an article in the newspaper, Mum,' James looks down, his voice drops, 'with a photograph of me, in my scout uniform.'

Most of the boys, who'd started in the Beaver and Cub scouts when James was little, had given up. It was seen as babyish or uncool or they'd gone on to join other things. James and David and a couple of their friends had stayed on because they loved the trips. Their leader was a tough old ex-policeman who expected a lot out of them and got it. He also gave them more freedom then they had with their parents. Similar to the Duke of Edinburgh awards, the Queen Scout award is a challenge and they've nearly achieved it. But I know, and James knows, he'll be teased if this gets in the paper.

'Think of all the people who've helped you through this, James, your friends, the scouts, the people at the Para Olympics, the doctors, your teachers, so many people. This would be a chance for you to thank them publicly. Who knows, someone else out there, going through cancer, possibly facing an amputation, might read this article and have new hope.'

I can see the battle he's having with himself and know he'll be brave enough for this task, too.

Mum and Kenneth are delighted to hear about James' award. It's gratifying when other people recognise what grandparents have always known, that their grandchildren are wonderful. We spend pleasant minutes discussing David's excellent GCSE results and the recent concerts he's performed in with various groups. But Mum's distracted.

'I've heard from Delith.'

This would normally be headline news. Australia is so far away and Howard's sister, Delith, is so busy with three young children and her singing and teaching commitments, letters are never as frequent as Delith or her mum would like. Something's wrong.

'She's still not well and the doctors can't seem to figure out what the problem is.' Mum frowns. Surely, this can't be another tragedy. We must have had our quota for the time being.

'She's constantly tired.' This is definitely not like Delith, usually bubbling with energy.

'And she's having awful pain in her joints, especially her hands.' For a singing teacher, who has to play the piano all day, this is a serious problem.

'Could it be some kind of arthritis?' I wonder out loud. Certainly, Mum and Howard have had problems with this.

'They're doing tests. One doctor mentioned Lupus. I guess we just have to wait and see.' Not a happy prospect. I make a mental note to try to find out more about Lupus.

*

The autumn term starts. James has to apply to the universities he'd like to go to next year.

'Mum, I can't decide if I want to be a doctor or a film director.'

This isn't as mad as it seems. James is bright and caring. He's always excelled in the sciences and been good with people. He's seen plenty of hospitals from the 'other side of the bed'. But he also loves films and all the business that goes with them. He and David have a vast collection of film magazines that they've read cover to cover.

'James, I can't make this decision for you.' We'd been persuaded to give him advice about what subjects to study at GCSE level and were blamed for every bad day he had for those two years.

'All I can say is that I'm sure you'll be good at whatever you choose. Becoming a doctor would be very hard work. You would have to be fully committed. But Steven Spielberg's mum probably wanted him to get a proper job, when he was your age, too.'

He decides on medicine and agonises over the application forms. There are yet more rumours of big changes for Howard at work. I begin to look for deputy headship posts and David becomes the musical director of a local pantomime group. He also takes an extra RSA computing course, writes a film and video column for the college magazine and develops his own film website.

After nearly a year of discussing what James wants to do to celebrate his special eighteenth birthday, it ends up being quite low-key. It's the first birthday in three years that he isn't in hospital and we all seem to have developed a 'keeping our heads down' mentality. We have a small family party then he trips off out on the town with his friends.

We worry about the 'drink culture' that seems to exist amongst young people. James in particular has a very low tolerance to drink, probably because his body weight is reduced by at least a fifth compared to his taller, two legged peers. The doctors also warn him that his liver and other organs have already had more than their share of abuse, from the chemotherapy, and he should go easy. The only reassurance we have is the universally agreed point that, amongst their friends, the nominated driver does not drink.

*

'Mum, I've got an interview at Cambridge!' James looks both excited and alarmed. 'I'll need a suit.' He hurries off to consult his friends and figure out how to prepare.

I'm delighted that this news seems to have dispelled James' deep disappointment at receiving a rejection from another university. We're told some places reject anyone who has also applied to Oxford or Cambridge. I'm not sure of the logic of this but then I've never been involved in the process before.

James' college runs seminars in Oxbridge preparation and I'm proud enough for tears when he sets off with his dad on the interview day. I hurry home from school eager to hear all about it.

'Cambridge is a wonderful place,' Howard tells me.

'They have porters and the buildings are so old and so beautiful.' I can hear the longing in James' descriptions. 'But I made a mess of the interview.' A dark shadow crosses my son's face.

'You can't know that, James. Everyone's bound to be nervous and make mistakes.' But I can see I haven't convinced him.

We don't have to wait long for the letter. The college are sorry they don't have a place to offer James but they'll put him in the 'pool'. This is a collection of worthy overspill students looking for spare spots in other colleges within Cambridge University. This is a very long shot and we're quickly told there's nothing for him.

When two more rejections come through, James is distraught.

'This is worse than having cancer,' he cries in despair. 'Everyone else has had offers. Rory's had five! Why am I not good enough?'

Most of his friends also have girlfriends and I can see the fears he had before the amputation are being confirmed in his mind.

'For a start, James, none of your friends have applied to do medicine. You know it's much harder to get into than most other subjects.'

'It's that B in physics,' James says with finality.

'When we interview for jobs, it can be the tiniest thing that separates candidates. If you have a lot of good people but only one place, it can be very hard to choose. Perhaps they're afraid your cancer will come back or medicine will be too physically demanding for you.' I'm desperate for him to know that he isn't being rejected as a person.

'If I'd gone to private school, I'd have had a better chance. It's your fault. I've missed out because you care more about money then my future.' James glares at me. It's his frustration speaking and he knows this isn't true. We've had this discussion before. One of his friends is a day pupil at a prestigious fee-paying school.

'If that's the reason they've rejected you then it's their foolish mistake and you shouldn't want to have anything to do with a place like that.' Unfairness always makes my blood boil. 'If these people can't appreciate what you've achieved under the most difficult circumstances, then they don't deserve to have you in their university.'

This makes James pause and think. 'Ravi has had a load of rejections, as well. He's had all top grades and he's come from one of the hardest, most deprived areas of Huddersfield.' James shakes his head.

I cannot understand why these mysterious university bodies, sitting somewhere in an ivory tower, can't see the value there is in pure strength of character.

I phone my father and brother, to investigate the possibility of James going to study in Arizona or Michigan, where they live. While people in England are protesting about having to pay £1000 tuition, we discover it would cost $14-15,000 a year for tuition in the US. Additionally, James' on-going medical and living expenses would have to be paid for.

Finally, after weeks of watching James smile and congratulate all of his friends, he receives an offer from Leeds University. He'll be studying in the very hospitals he was a patient in. I suspect someone there put in a good word for him. He's relieved but a little disappointed.

'It's so close,' he says.

And so familiar, I suspect he's thinking. James longs to leave home and get out into the world.

I'm selected for interview for a deputy headship post. As part of the process I'm asked do a fifteen-minute presentation on "a recent piece of work, of which I'm proud, that demonstrates my educational philosophy and includes a discussion of how I would disseminate the good practice throughout the school community". I'm very nervous sitting on my little wooden chair, while six pairs of eyes study me from behind a semi-circle of tables. But the passion I feel for the work I'm doing carries me through and I get the job.

I'll be the deputy head of a nursery and infant school, with approximately 130 children plus a 48-place nursery. It's in a delightful village on the edge of the moors and the headteacher seems lovely. When she originally showed me around the school, before I applied, she'd had something specific and positive to say about every member of staff and the walls were covered in the clearly cherished work of the children. Very excited about the prospect of this change; I'm also a little frightened of leaving the friends and security of a school I've worked in for twelve years.

We bask in the pleasure of this new opportunity for a week before we receive a phone call from Australia to say that Delith has a brain tumour and only two months to live.

*

It's very early morning on a school day, when that phone call comes. My body feels stiffly robotic as I go through the motions to get ready for work.

It isn't possible. I picture my sister-in-law, all four foot ten inches of her and know this can't be real. As if compressing her life force into such a tiny body made it brighter, more powerful, she always sparkles with energy. She has the gift of listening with her whole self, a gift that makes you feel valued and loved. Two years older than Howard, Delith already lived in London when I joined the family so I haven't spent a lot of time with her but she's still precious to me.

I remember the way she hugged me as a sister when we first met and the incredible night I watched her perform in the opera, *Yeoman of the Guard*, with Tommy Steel on the grass beneath the Tower of London. Along with other family members, I've seen her sing many times. Her pure soprano notes can raise goose bumps up my arms. Her stage presence is natural and mesmerising.

In James' room, I seek out the kangaroo toy she lovingly made for him during long hours of rehearsals. And a photo recalls the time the brothers and sisters clubbed together to fly Delith home from Australia as a surprise gift for Mum's sixtieth birthday. I can't help but smile when I remember how Mum thought we'd bought her a dog when the duvet cover, with Delith inside, moved. I can hear haunting echoes of the Christmas carols we filled the pub with after the party.

David quietly says, 'What can you expect, Mum? We have a big family, more people to love but more to lose, too.'

Howard, his mum, brothers and remaining sister are by Delith's side within a week. In the face of this mass determination, they manage to persuade the doctors to at least try radiotherapy. They're able to share some lovely times together and help Delith's husband, Arthur, sort out some of the overwhelming problems facing them.

Back home, Howard feels the situation is grim but not entirely hopeless. He has remarkable stories to tell of giant spiders, lizards, bats, leeches and incredible, strange fruits. He's also covered in bug bites. Delith lives in a beautiful place, high in the mountains above Toowoomba, steamy, hot and full of extraordinary trees. Howard particularly enjoyed getting to know our niece and two nephews whilst he was there. There is concern in his observations of Mum, though. This latest blow has really shaken her. She struggled to concentrate in Australia and was often anxious and forgetful.

Coping with all of this, thoughts about my new job, writing reports and finishing up things at my old school leave me tense. My headteacher asks me to rewrite 39 pages of my reports, as she feels they're too 'jargony' (I must still be in job application mode) then she has a go at me about the discipline in my classroom. This seems to come out of the blue but perhaps in the fog I'm in I haven't noticed. It feels like steel toe caps in the ribs from my position on the floor. A few days later, she asks me to take three days off. Feeling a fraud, I try to decline but she insists.

It's enough to help me complete a few tasks, get a healthier sleep pattern back and prepare for the next big changes in our lives.

*

Delith completes her first course of radiotherapy and the scans show her tumour has shrunk by 50%. They follow this with another 3-day intensive course of radiation through her eye. Much as James and my cousin Sherry's experiences had been, there are extreme highs and desperate lows.

We keep in touch by phone. Each week brings new hardships and kindnesses from friends, neighbours and members of their church family. People help with the nitty-gritty of day to day requirements; driving the children to places they need to be, preparing meals on a daily rota, gifts of prayer, money, time and support. There are mistakes made in medications, difficulty in communicating with doctors, financial problems and hundreds of miles to travel for treatments.

This latest trauma has a catastrophic effect on Howard's mum. Enduring the struggles of her grandchild had been agony. Losing her beautiful daughter, Louise, so tragically and suddenly, just as James began to improve, was unbearable. Kenneth worries because he doesn't think Mum's been able to cry for Louise, yet. Mum's forgetful and distant. Now, torn between being with her daughter and becoming an extra burden for Delith's family or trying to cope with the image of Delith suffering so far away, Mum pays a great price physically, mentally and emotionally.

Despite this latest hurricane in our lives, we still have to 'get on and do', as they say here. James is awarded a bronze medal in the British Olympiad. We'd never even heard of this. Apparently, only a student with a modular average of 95% or above in A-level Biology is eligible to sit the demanding exam. I travel to London with my amazing son to attend the ceremony.

It's hard to afford this news much attention, though, as we learn that our good friend, Linda, mother of one of James' best friends, Alex, is diagnosed with breast cancer. She'd been struggling with an extremely difficult situation at work, for a year or two prior to this, so no one was terribly surprised or alarmed by her loss of weight, tiredness or the dulling of her skin and hair. It's far too late when they discover the magnitude of what's happening inside her body.

I visit her, as soon as I hear the news, taking some Coenzyme Q10's in my desperation to do something. She looks relieved to see me, as if I might really be able to help.

'How did James do it?' she asks. I can see she's overwhelmed.

'One day at a time, Linda. Just try to keep hoping.' These words sound stupid and hopelessly inadequate. I tell her about the supplements I've brought and about the gloomy prognoses my aunt and James had been given. But the fear never leaves her face.

Within a fortnight of her diagnosis, she is dead.

Her funeral's on Good Friday and is a beautiful and moving service. Alex reads a heartbreaking poem which he's written. I wonder where this seventeen-year-old finds his courage and strength. The same boys who stood beside James now have another friend to support.

The two weeks of the Easter holidays are spent sorting through the twelve years worth of accumulated 'stuff' I've brought home from my old school then transferring anything of use to my new classroom. Before I know it, I'm a deputy head and people are coming to me for decisions and advice.

Being the up-front, say-what-I-think, foot-in-the-mouth sort of person I am, it's not a smooth or easy transition. Responsible for driving through change, I'm not expecting to be popular but it's difficult to feel on the outside and to sometimes walk a tightrope between the headteacher and the staff. Most of the people are lovely, though. My new boss is calm, patient and always supportive. Together we begin to work towards our vision for the school.

We make a good team. I storm into her office, ranting and raving about something that's happened and she listens calmly then tells me that she understands but doesn't think we'll say it quite like that. She soon has me giggling then we work out how to tackle the problem.

Howard and I meet monthly for long walks with two of my teaching friends from my old school and their husbands. They listen, with their shared educational experience, to my tortuous tales, allowing me to vent my frustrations and celebrate my successes.

One of the first times I'm on the other side of the interviewing process, we appoint a talented young woman who also happens to be a Christian. Jill becomes my classroom assistant. I've worked alongside other Christians before but not like her. She's open about her faith and happy to discuss our respective journeys. For the first time ever, I discover the power of having someone to pray with at work. She's an artist and knows God in a very visual way, which helps me to see him in new ways, too.

One image she shares with me is of asking God for his advice but with her fingers in her ears and making a funny noise to drown out the answer she knows is right but doesn't want to hear. I can relate to that picture and we laugh at our foolishness and wonder at God's tolerance.

One morning, she bursts into the classroom.

'You'll never guess what happened to me on the way to work.' Jill is glowing.

I stop to listen.

'I'm just standing at the bus stop, next to this woman, minding my own business, when I feel I'm supposed to offer her a polo mint.' She grins at the silliness of this thought.

'I start arguing in my head, "I can't do that. She'll think I'm barking mad!"' Jill throws her hands up.

'But the thought won't go away. Finally, I give in and take the mints out of my bag and hold them out to her. It's amazing. The woman takes a sweet and pours out all the fear and anxiety she has because she's on her way to a job interview.'

I look at Jill and feel the hairs stand up on my arms. The rest of the world might think we're foolish and deluded but I'm thrilled to think that God can use us like this to help strangers, to know he cares about the details of people's lives. *But he punishes your son for nothing.*

I'm ready for the summer holidays, when they finally arrive. Howard and I take part in two charity walks, including a ten-mile 'beer walk'. This involves over 1000 walkers, in themed, costumed teams, going from pub to pub whilst the children who line the streets, throw money into our collecting buckets.

James finishes his final exams in college and David, his end of module tasks and tests. We have a family holiday in Minorca and James also has a wild, 18–30's holiday in Tenerife with his friends.

By the end of the summer we learn that Delith has improved so much she's even managed to cook a meal and do some laundry for her family. Considering I often complain about similar tasks, I realise they're actually things I should be grateful for.

Howard's promoted to a directorship. The company's so keen to have him back on the board that they offer him the position on his own terms. He'll only have to make occasional trips to Stratford and they'll come to Bradford to see him some of the time.

The boys get their college results and have done extremely well. Together with two other friends, they complete the final challenge towards their Queen Scout awards; a fifty-mile walk in the Lake District over three days. They've organised it all themselves and come home with a real sense of achievement. James has open blisters on his hands from his crutches and other places where his artificial leg has rubbed.

In September, we have a 'circus' party for our friends. Everyone has to come in costume prepared to perform their 'act'. We have a fantastic time. One couple come as harlequins and amaze us by their skilful use of a Diablo. There's 'The International Man of Mystery' whose costume includes wearing a waste paper basket on his head (the zone of incomprehension). Then he's able, with the help of his lovely assistant, to work out which numbers the audience has chosen by consulting his 'runes' (cutlery). There's a clown on a unicycle, a lion that can tell jokes and do tricks, even without a lion-tamer, and many more. I do a tightrope act with a safety net, zero feet off the ground, in a tutu and stripy tights.

Our boys and their friends prepare hot dogs, candyfloss, popcorn and peanuts, do the bartending and serving. They look grown up in their waiter's uniforms and laugh at the embarrassing adults. Soon most of them, including James, will leave home for university.

Chapter 7

I shake the duvet into the new cover and smooth it over the single bed. The gold and brown geometric patterns don't do much to soften the institutional feel of the place. The building is old and probably as clean as it will ever be again until next summer. There is a smell of male hormones and training shoes. Between James' room and the one next door is a connecting wet room. It's so small, it's possible to shower and sit on the toilet at the same time. I wonder what the boy will be like who will share this intimate space with my son.

'Come on, Kimm, it's time to go.' Howard's voice is tender but firm. Howard, James and David are looking at me, as if I might suddenly fall apart. There isn't really enough space for the four of us in the long narrow room but I want to unpack all the boxes, make things tidy and straight. I am gently reminded that this will be James' home for the next nine months and he wants to organise it in his own way.

'You won't forget to ring this student support number and find out what they're offering?' I brush my hand across the large planner we bought for his desk. James has never been very good at organising his time or remembering dates and things. My insides quiver with worry and grief and surprise that my baby has become this young man so quickly. I'm not ready yet. We so nearly lost him, I can't ever imagine being able to let him go.

'He'll be fine,' Howard folds his arms around James, 'won't you, son?' His voice is husky and I realise, at last, I'm being self-indulgent.

We pick our way back through the clatter of voices and jumble of boxes that litter the corridor. The communal kitchen-sitting room for the ten boys in this unit is showing its age. We've already been shopping and claimed space in the cupboards and fridge.

'You will try to eat properly?' I can't stop myself. I know if I try to hold on too tight, I'll drive him away but somehow my brain and mouth have slipped their connections.

'I'll be OK, Mum.' At the touch of James' hand on my shoulder, the tears come. I'm glad he's behind me and can't see them.

I turn on the landing and crush him in a hug, then hurry down the stairs to the car. Forcing my face into a smile, I wave up at him.

James waves then hurries off to make new friends.

As usual, David's a great help to us, as we adjust to his brother's departure. ·It's wonderful to have our youngest son on his own at home for the first time. There's time to talk and listen to him without his noisy brother commanding all the attention, and he's interesting, thoughtful and very good company. David shares his dad's bizarre sense of humour. Being very practical and technically minded, we become dependent on him to keep all our 'machines' working and to help us with new computer software and such. I'm dreading the coming year when he too will be leaving us.

*

After initial improvements, Delith's health begins to decline in November, despite positive scan results. She's on medication for epilepsy, steroids for the inflammation in her brain and she's developed diabetes. Unable to drink the sweet drinks she craves, she becomes severely dehydrated in the extreme heat of the Australian summer. The tumour is growing again and there are real fears that it will spread to the brain stem, which causes excruciating pain. They're forced to try chemotherapy.

Through the dedication of her devoted husband, along with the love and support of their family, friends and church, they're able to keep Delith at home until the final week of her life, when she's mainly unconscious. The news of her death comes in March, just over a year after the original diagnosis.

Lorraine, having lost two sisters in a brief period of time, is suffering from depression and anxiety but feels she must be with Delith's family for the funeral. We hold a memorial service here on the same day and are able to download two pieces of music sung by Delith, to play in the church. There are nearly 600 people at the funeral in Australia and 120 people attend our memorial service.

At the front of the chapel we spread out the gorgeous quilt Delith made for her mother and place photographs, news clippings of her singing career and other mementos of her life. I feel numb, as we sit in the front row waiting for the service to start. The preacher's words are soothing but when Howard and his brothers each give a tribute tears just wash down my face. I open my mouth to sing the beautiful hymns but the words won't come and when Howard's voice falters, I cry some more. Mum's asked me to read the poem, *Immortality.* I pray I won't let her down, as I force my legs to carry me to the front. It must be the Spirit speaking the words through me because my insides have become fluid and insubstantial.

Afterwards, we move to the Sunday school rooms for refreshments and a chance to talk to the other mourners. The pure notes of Delith's voice bring her presence right among us. I feel a warm tired peace settle. It's as if my tears have cleaned the wound made when her life was ripped away. This opportunity to share memories, with other people who loved her, helps the healing to begin.

*

In and amongst this, Howard's company is sold again, to a European consortium. We're back to square one, as far as knowing what the future holds. To add to the déjà vu experience, I'm to have an OFSTED inspection at my new school, immediately after Easter, exactly a year after becoming deputy.

I'm also chosen as one of twelve teachers in our education authority (140 schools) to be an associate teacher of literacy. This means that other teachers can come and watch me teach or talk to me about related issues. I'm part of a team that meets regularly to discuss new initiatives in literacy. This certainly boosts my confidence, gives me a voice and adds weight to my impetus for change. The advisor that heads the team calls us 'experts' but I describe myself as an enthusiast.

*

Before we realised how rapidly Delith's health was deteriorating, Howard and I had arranged to visit her over Easter. Tied to school holidays, we were unable to move this forward when it became clear she wouldn't make it until then but still feel we want to continue with our plans.

Australia is a *long* way away. You don't really appreciate how far until you make that journey. It's a thirteen hour flight to our stopover in Singapore, after many hours of travel to get to London. Claustrophobia suffocates me and I want to climb over the other passengers by the time we arrive. Walking along the busy pavement in the evening, I begin to appreciate what a privilege it is to experience the exotic sights, sounds and smells of other countries.

Singapore is liquid with humidity but very clean; there are hefty fines for things like chewing gum in public places. The people we meet are unfailingly polite and helpful. We eat strange, delicious food; wander for miles looking at the shops, parks and other sights. There are unusual, extravagant, scented flowers everywhere. We treat ourselves to 'high tea' at Raffles and imagine we're in an old movie. When the heat finally beats us, we relax in the rooftop pool and sip Singapore Slings, continuing the Hollywood feel.

The first five days in Australia we spend in Port Douglas at the Thala Beach Resort. What a glorious place. Our 'room' is like a tree house built into the hillside on stilts, with a balcony from which we can look out over the canopy of the rainforest to the sea beyond. The warm air is heavy with the perfume of flowers and the sound of strange birds, insects and the sea.

We revel in our exploration of this corner of the world. We feel like Tarzan or Indiana Jones as we hike up a verdant, rainforest trail in the Mossman Gorge, tempted by the vines that hang around us but alert for dangers. The air smells rich and earthy. Our skin leaks in the steamy heat.

I can sense excitement in the tension of Howard's body, the animation of his speech. He can't sit still, as we glide over the ocean to the Great Barrier Reef. He is desperate to share this undreamt of aspiration with me so, despite an unreasonable fish phobia, I climb into flippers and snorkelling gear and sit on the platform, my legs dangling in the warm sea. But, when I put my face in the water, the colours, variety and movement of the fish leap into vivid life around me, and my determination is replaced by utter panic. I return my equipment, encourage Howard to do the proper diving he longs for and see the life of the reef from the safety of a glass submersible.

We can almost feel David Attenborough beside us as we travel up to the 'tablelands' on the Skyrail cable car. Mesmerised by the wonder and variety of the creatures and plants we see, from the brilliant blue butterflies as big as my hand to the python we have to carefully step past on our way to breakfast, we decide God must have had a lot of fun creating Australia.

From there we travel to Toowoomba, via Brisbane. At last, I can meet the people and see the places that Delith had written so lovingly about over the years and share in fellowship at the church that are such a support to the family. There is something very special about visiting another country from the 'inside', not as a tourist but in the homes of people that live there. We feel blessed to have time to spend with this part of our family.

*

Arriving home, tired and jetlagged, the house smells of beer and boys. James and David won't meet our eyes. They've had a forbidden party and are clearly shaken by how easily it got out of hand. But they've done their best to put the house straight. There's no lasting damage, nothing carpet and upholstery cleaner won't fix.

I stumble off to the supermarket to stock up on essentials. My brain feels full of cogs all spinning at different speeds, filling my head with clouds of dust and noise. I stand in the brightly-lit fruit and veg section and try to remember what I need, what the coming week will involve. A neon OFSTED warning sign flashes unhelpfully in my mind.

'Hello.'

My eyes take a moment to adjust to looking outwards. A short, bustley woman stands in front of me. She's one of the childminders who collect strings of children from school each day.

'Hi, sorry, I've just come back from holiday. I'm not really with it.' I smile and try to dredge up her name.

'I wondered why you weren't at the funeral.'

I don't trust my sluggish brain and can't think what she's talking about.

'You haven't heard.' She pauses to look at me. 'Amy died. Stan's little girl.'

Immediately, I see the timid seven-year-old, her fine blonde hair and open Down's syndrome smile. Everyone loved Amy. Then I think of Stan, my colleague and friend. He and his wife adopted two Down's children, then had ·a boy of their own. Stan gave up a lucrative law practice and retrained as a primary teacher to have more time with his family.

I sway, darkness creeps round the edges of my vision. I want to sit down.

'How? Why?' It doesn't make sense. Two weeks ago Amy was playing and running, sharing her shy smile. I think wistfully of all the long years when no-one I knew died.

'It was her heart. She'd been in the garden with the family and ran inside to get something. At the top of the stairs she dropped dead. It was a lovely funeral…'

The woman keeps talking but I'm stunned and can't seem to hear. Amy's little brothers both come to our school, what will they make of it all? And her parents, I can't bear to imagine how they must be feeling.

Grief certainly puts school inspections into perspective. We are a very subdued community, as we come together after the break. But irrespective of our tragic loss, this OFSTED experience is entirely different to my previous one. Significantly, my headteacher has confidence in our school's strengths, is aware of our weaknesses and prepared to discuss the strategies we've identified to make improvements. This attitude of looking forward to the inspection, as a possible tool for improvement, filters through to everyone else. Plus, we've all been here before.

The inspector admits that he arrived expecting to give us a poor report based on dismal results in the SAT tests before I came to the school. However, he's impressed by our self-assessments, the improvements we've already made and our plans for moving ahead. He happily lends his weight, via his report and suggested action points, to all that we want to do. Far from coming away from the inspection feeling deflated and exhausted, we're able to steam ahead with renewed vigour.

*

We discover that David needs glasses for long distance and he looks quite handsome and grown up at six foot two, wearing trendy specs. He makes us smile with exclamations like, "Wow! I didn't know leaves looked like that!"

Just before his eighteenth birthday, David passes his driving test first time and follows it with the extra Pass Plus lessons his brother had. With James home for the summer, I have to queue up to use my own car. I don't really mind. It's lovely to have their company, when they take me to work so they can have 'wheels' for the day.

The boys agree to go on holiday with us to visit family in America. Having James home and spending time with so many of the people I love is wonderful. My four-year-old nephew, whom I've not seen for three years, meets us in the car park of my brother's condominium.

'Hiya Kimm, how are ya?' he says and I know I'm loved despite the distance. Howard's in his element with all the children to play with and the copious amounts of hero-worship are soaked up quite happily by my sons.

We hurry back to Britain for David's results day.

*

We drive down out of the Pennines and into the flat farmland of Lincolnshire. The car is packed with David's things, the few gaps stuffed with our separate thoughts. I feel like I'm headed toward a partial execution, a 'bemothering', the severing of a hugely important part of my life. I know I'll survive but there'll be a gaping wound.

Lincoln Cathedral appears atop the only hill for miles around, the city spilling down and spreading out on the plains below. We snake along amongst the other families bringing their children to university for the first time. David had done well in his A-level exams and carefully researched which university would best meet his needs. Intensely practical, he'd chosen this hands-on media production course on a relatively small city campus.

As much as he dreads change, David never needed any prompting or encouragement or advice to organise this next big step in his life.

'Mum, I want to do it myself,' David tells me firmly, as I start to organise his things.

'Have you got a list of what we need to buy?' Howard steps in to take the sting out of the moment. 'We'll grab a bite to eat and then leave you to get settled, David.'

Only my son's manic fidgeting and the way he pushes the pizza around his plate lets me know how he's feeling. I reach up to hug him goodbye and his skinny frame is all elbows and angles in my arms. It's a quiet ride home.

The consortium that bought Howard's company insisted on buying back all of our shares. This turns out to be a huge blessing, as within five months the company is placed in the hands of the receivers. Howard and four other senior men work extremely hard to put together a bid for a new management buyout. With the money we received for our shares and after months of stress, heartache and effort, we become part owners of a large retail company, at the same time safeguarding the jobs of over eight hundred people and minimising the impact on the suppliers that Howard had known and worked with for so many years.

Our lives are full and the busy-ness helps me to give the boys their freedom and independence. I try to limit my phone calls to once a week and unsuccessfully try to refrain from interfering, nagging and offering unwanted advice. But there are still gaps in my centre. We continue to play badminton every Friday night, go to a fitness club, take part in charitable and social events, enjoy walking weekends and visit our boys from time to time. I settle into my role as a deputy.

On one walk with friends in the Lake District we're soaked to the skin, through layers of 'waterproof' clothing, on a blustery autumn day. Climbing mountains in the fresh air and glorious colours are some compensation. And hot baths are that much more special when I'm cold, wet and muddy. I also feel I've earned that portion of Sticky Toffee Pudding with butterscotch sauce.

Thankfully, James continues to be free from cancer. He's doing very well with his medical studies despite finding it hard to manage a social life that involves a great deal of drinking and, it turns out, smoking. I can only rage and pray about what I see as his headlong push towards self-destruction.

Howard loves becoming one of the owners of the company. The response from his employees and their corner of the business community is all very positive. He likes and respects his partners and is glad to be free of the often unrealistic demands of aloof owners and 'The City'. There are a few difficult teething problems at the beginning but they're able to face and solve them as a team. At last, they're free to tackle the things they see as problems and use their significant collective experience to re-build their business.

We don't get to choose our blessings in this life. Given the choice between financial security and having our loved ones or James' leg back, would be a 'no-brainer'. Having managed for many years, quite happily, with very little money, I'm uncertain and a bit uncomfortable about our improved circumstances. The Bible has quite a few warnings for those who are well off, the most famous the one about the camel and the eye of the needle. I still find it hard to spend money and worry that people will view us differently. Happily, Howard and I have a mutual desire to share our blessings and not let our circumstances change the people we are.

One benefit we do enjoy is taking wonderful holidays. Howard's neck and shoulder pain have flared up again as a result of all the stress of the buyout and I feel trapped in a tiny, miserable, dark place in my head. In the Easter holidays we treat ourselves to ten days in the Seychelles. Gradually, the warm, smiling people, glorious sunshine and gentle breezes weave their spell and coax us from our impatient, wound up lives. We feel so much better; I wonder if I could get another trip on prescription.

The islands are incredibly beautiful and often seen in films, like *Castaway* or adverts, like the Bounty Bar ones. The people are descended from French and English 'conquerors', freed slaves that had no way to return to their native African villages, and other sea-faring folk that had fallen in love with the place. The food and language reflect these varied influences.

While there, Howard takes the exam for his PADI certificate, to enable him to do more adventurous scuba diving. He studies all week and has several training sessions before the big underwater exam. One of the things he has to do is dive to 16 metres and, when asked, remove his mask then replace it. Because of his contact lenses he'll have to keep his eyes closed so will, in effect, be totally cut off from the instructor.

Once the signal's given, Howard takes the mask away but accidentally breathes water in through his nose, for a split second. Unable to speak, hear, see, breathe or surface quickly enough, he's terrified. Suddenly, he hears in his memory the first rule of diving – don't panic. As he steadies his mind, he remembers what to do and is soon looking into the face of his very relieved instructor.

I have a long-standing and unreasonable fear of fish so diving holds no appeal for me and Howard's experience does nothing to alter my opinion, either. I spend the time he's away, ensconced on a sun lounger, under an umbrella, with a book. I do venture into the bath-water-warm, crystal clear sea but only as far as I can see the white sand under my toes. For some reason, I'm not afraid of the shy angelfish that rush to play round me, attracted by my pink swimsuit.

Back home, we decide to move house. Although our old house was ideal while the boys were growing up, there are niggling little things that we want to change. Chief among them is the fact that the garden gets hardly any sunshine apart from when it's directly overhead. We find an old farmhouse, like the ones we dreamed about in our youth, and fall in love with it.

We have a mad panic to finish all those jobs round the house that we endlessly put off, and then sell it to the first people who come to view. This is followed by more frenetic activity, packing, organising changes of address, trips and phone calls to estate agents, mortgage lenders, lawyers, insurers, etc.

*

'Declan, that's enough. Oliver, are you listening?' The usual suspects are clustered at the far edge of the carpet, doing just enough whispering, pinching and squirming to distract and annoy everyone else. This part of the lesson is drawing to a close. We need to recap, tidy up and move on to the next tasks.

'Ross, Declan, Sky, sit down.' Their misbehaviour is escalating. Three of them have bounced to their feet engrossed in an argument. I'd split them up, named them, tried to draw them into the activity but they're lost to me now, in their own little battle. My classroom support assistant, Sue, has done what she can to settle them but to no effect. With a sigh, I stand up and wade through the sensible children, sitting patiently and eager to learn.

'You sit next to Jonathan and he'll show you how to listen carefully.' I gently turn Declan and point him toward one corner of the carpet away from the other trouble makers. Then I repeat the procedure with Sky, sending her to an opposite corner.

Reaching down I grab the knees of Oliver, an easily distracted little boy who wears glasses and doesn't listen or concentrate well, sitting at the furthest edge of the carpet in the midst of this challenging crowd. I look up and speak to the group, whilst I gently pull this child forward to a place in the centre of the carpet where I hope he'll be able to see and concentrate better. Because I'm trying to make eye contact with each child, I don't notice that Oliver has flopped backwards, like a rag doll. When my gaze sweeps down to take him in, I realise he has a tiny carpet burn, the size of a 5p, on his back and a smaller one on his wrist.

I'm devastated. I've devoted my working life to helping children and am appalled to have inadvertently hurt this boy. Immediately, I ask Sue to supervise and rush Oliver to first aid and record the details in the accident book. And I pray.

Back in the classroom, I'm given the peace to remain calm and normal for the children, despite the chills shivering through me from the shock. Oliver doesn't seem to be upset at all and works quite happily next to me. At the first opportunity, I ask Sue if she felt I'd over-reacted to the situation or behaved heavy-handedly. But she tells me that she's comfortable that it had merely been an unfortunate accident. I inform my headteacher and my union, fully aware of the litigious culture we live in.

Sweating, my hands trembling, I speak to Oliver's mum when she comes to collect him at the end of the day. When I've told her what happened, I explain that if she's in any way unhappy she's welcome to speak with the ·headteacher and/or the other adult who was present.

A strange cat's-got-the-cream smile slides over her face. She collects her son without a glance at the marks and sweeps out the door.

I know I'm in trouble. Two years earlier, I'd taught Oliver in his first year of full time education and had problems with the family then. The father had been instructing his four-year-old son to hit other children when they hurt him. We had several discussions, in which I tried to explain that 95% of the time, bumps and knocks were entirely accidental with children crashing into each other due to undeveloped gross motor skills. I also patiently went through our behaviour and bullying policies and strategies, trying to reassure him that all incidents were dealt with carefully and fully. He wouldn't accept any of it.

More recently, we discovered that the father had been telling him to hit a younger, autistic child. Oliver was observed, on more than one occasion by more than one person, chasing and taunting the autistic child. When his victim lashed out in frustration, Oliver would inform his parents that he was being bullied.

The most telling incident was when Oliver had been caught throwing ice and snow at other children in the playground. The rule was he would have to miss his playtimes the next day. He came into school in the morning, screaming the place down. When I went out to see if I could help, the father told me Oliver was upset about missing playtime. I looked at the child and explained, for the father's sake, that I was sure his dad would want us to keep children in, if they had thrown ice at him. We could not allow children to hurt others and he had known what the rules were before he went out to play.

When I offered to take Oliver into the classroom, he screamed even louder and the father informed me that he wasn't having his son upset like this so I left them to it and returned to the classroom. About twenty minutes later, the child sauntered in with a big grin on his face and accepted his punishment quite happily. In the afternoon, I asked him what had changed his mind and was told he'd been given a large quantity of sweets. This was possibly one of the worst families to fall foul of.

*

Parenting is a complex and incredibly important skill, sadly not mastered by all. As families become busier, snatching meals at different times, often in front of the television, and increasingly children are encouraged to watch DVDs or play on computers alone in their bedrooms, many are arriving in school with very poor speaking and listening skills.

The most amazing example of this was a little boy, from an English-speaking family, who seemed to have an extremely limited vocabulary. After months of complaints from people that he was swearing all the time and discussions with his mother, who asserted that he never heard words like that at home, I slowly began to realise that the child didn't know what we meant when we asked him not to swear. Eventually, bright red and cringing with embarrassment, I took him out into the corridor and told him exactly which words he mustn't say. When we finally had a swear-free day, and I happily announced that fact to his mum at the school gates; her reply was, "Bloody hell!"

A more disturbing incident happened with another child as we returned to school from a day trip to the zoo. He was an underachieving, six-year-old boy with few friends. I sat with him on the bus and tried to encourage him to talk about the things he'd seen and done during our excursion. It was very hard work; most of his responses were monosyllabic, delivered with almost weary resignation. As we neared our destination, we passed the local video shop and instantly he became animated and enthusiastic. He could barely speak fast enough in his effort to tell me all the gruesome details of the horror films, classified for 18+, he'd watched from that shop.

There was another child who was clearly being abused but despite every effort we seemed unable to help. On her first day of school she stood wailing, rigid and petrified in the corner of the room, where her mother had pushed her through the door. In the end, I gently but firmly lifted her over to the carpet, where the other children were, and sat her with the nursery teachers I hoped she'd be familiar with. Over the months that followed, I watched her lovely character unfold as she went from being a pathetic mute to a lively, smiley little girl in the classroom. Her countenance would change abruptly when she was collected from school each day.

We'd been told that the grandfather had sexually abused the mother as a child, yet she often left this child in his care. We logged every mark on her body, every incident of worrying behaviour and reported our concerns to all the appropriate bodies but nothing seemed to be done. I lost patience one day and told the mother her excuses for the child's poor attendance weren't good enough but I'm afraid it probably did more harm than good. I ought to have tried harder to cultivate a partnership with the woman. Eventually, they moved away so perhaps we had been making progress.

Another child came from a home which had been raided by police looking for drugs; prostitution was hinted at. They found squalor, a dwelling with little furniture, no food and filth of every description on all the surfaces. He was the middle of six children, by different fathers. His sister and brother brought him to school or he came by himself, never accompanied by an adult.

I taught him in year two, as he approached seven years of age. He'd had very poor attendance up until then but began, slowly, to come more regularly and to make improvements. I persuaded the Educational Social Worker to bring his mum in to look at his work. When she came, I enthused over his progress, praised his improved attendance and showed her his writing and drawings. She took a brief glance, and in front of the child, announced that it was 'crap' then walked out. By the time he reached junior school he was regularly excluded for violent, aggressive behaviour.

These were just a few of the extreme cases. Most of the hundreds of children that I've taught over the years have been within a broad range of happy, healthy, well-adjusted boys and girls. Their parents have cared for and about them to the best of their ability. Many infant and nursery school teachers wish that the 'great powers that be' would pay more attention to the observations and concerns of the professionals involved in the Early Years sector. If only more could be done while the children are still young and before any more damage is inflicted, perhaps there wouldn't be so many desperate problems later on.

*

My fears are confirmed when two uniformed police officers walk across the back of the hall while I'm leading assembly, the following day. Oliver's mum had gone straight to the child protection unit. She wants me crucified.

Over a hundred small children and a handful of adults watch me, as my heart thunders but words keep coming out of my stiffly smiling mouth. I know God is with me and wildly wonder what He has in store for me in prison.

The police speak briefly to my headteacher, Judith, and satisfied that I am not a danger to anyone, they quietly leave. Judith is fantastic. She makes endless phone calls, registers complaints that the parents hadn't followed procedure, as they'd been advised, and insists that a decision be made within a week so that the nightmare won't be hanging over our heads throughout the upcoming half term holiday. The other members of staff give me their unqualified support, even the ones I'd had prickly encounters with previously.

I hear, 'There but for the grace of God…' float down the stairs, followed by heartfelt murmurs of agreement. We'd all seen teachers hounded through the media, heard about careers and lives destroyed in a moment of snapped temper, a careless action or an error of judgement.

It's been a very long day. At home, I phone Jill. She left our school a few months earlier for a different job.

Jill listens carefully and offers no platitudes.

'Shall we pray?'

'Over the phone?' It's such an unexpected response. A giddy giggle bubbles through me.

'Why not?'

Smiling, I close my eyes and let Jill's words soothe me. It feels as if a balloon full of liquid peace has burst on top of my head and the warm contents flow over me.

· I thank God for the revelation of the respect people have and the support they offer me. It seems a very long week and I know that for many other teachers caught in this situation it can drag on for months or even years. On Friday, we're informed that neither the police nor social services will be pursuing the case. It'll be up to the parents to make a formal complaint to the school.

Although I'm exonerated, the parents keep their son at home for some weeks after the incident until they receive an official warning that he has to attend school. Each morning I can feel a ball of anxiety swell in my gut, as I wonder what will happen when we meet again. Having prayed for the family and myself, I'm relieved to find that, when they finally appear, I'm able to behave quite normally, smiling and welcoming Oliver back. I feel no animosity for the boy, just pity for the lessons he's being taught at home.

I'm not surprised to learn later that they're still pursuing a case for compensation. Nor am I particularly shocked when another child in the class asks me if I'll be going to prison soon. Oliver had apparently been jubilantly telling his friends 'down the pub' that the police would be taking me away.

I can't help but recall the number of children I have reported my fears for, obvious cases of prolonged physical cruelty, abuse and neglect, when nothing seems to be done. Yet a simple accident, witnessed and openly reported, brings down the full weight of the police and social services. A headteacher, in the news at the time, was subjected to eight punches in the face by a parent, angry that her son had been excluded for taking a knife to another child. The parent only received a warning. Children are vulnerable and need our protection, teachers are in a position of huge responsibility and mustn't be allowed to harm the children in their care but sometimes common sense and balance seem to be missing. I thank God that it prevailed in my case.

*

Summer 2001

In the midst of the trauma of the assault charge, preparing to move house, working full time and general chaos happening around us, we host the wedding reception of Howard's cousin, Michael, and his lovely bride, Ellie. After a long and, I suspect, often lonely search, he's found his perfect match and we're thrilled for them both. Howard works slavishly to get our garden looking its best, we borrow an extra gazebo, put up balloons and the ever wonderful Pat loans us five pots of beautiful white lilies. We prepare enough food to barbeque for the fifty guests and are very thankful, when the weather stays dry after a week's rain.

The house move goes quite smoothly, especially for me, as I just tootle off for the last day of school and leave Howard, the boys and the removal firm to do the work. My turn comes in the first week of the summer break, which I spend unpacking the house and packing for our holiday.

Matthew and his family are visiting when we return. It's fun to catch up with our three young nieces and strange to have girls around. But Matthew and Alison are anxious to speak to Howard and me on our own.

'Mum's much worse since the last time we saw her.'

Defensiveness frizzles up my spine. How dare they swoop in twice a year from London and tell us what's what with Mum.

'It's just the stress of coping with so many visitors,' I suggest. 'She's had so much to bear over the last few years.'

Dismay flashes across their faces but they don't push. I know they both love Mum so, although I want to resist what they're saying, I reluctantly take off the blinkers of familiarity. They're right. Mum is more forgetful, she repeats phrases over and over. The unrelenting traumas have pummelled the very rocks of her foundations, reducing them to sand and the sand is beginning to shift. We don't want to think what it might mean. Kenneth agrees to take her to the doctor.

On the first of September, I join my friends, Pat and Christine, to run the Flora Light Challenge in Hyde Park, London. It's a 5000 metre run, for women, and we'll be raising money for Macmillan Cancer Research. Nerves get the better of my bladder and I spend anxious minutes queued outside the porta-loos. It's terrific fun being one of 23,000 women doing aerobics in the park then lining up, anxious to get underway. There are so many people that it takes me ten minutes to get to the starting line once the race has begun. It's humbling to see all the good causes represented and we're grateful for the supporters and entertainers that encourage us as we slog along. There is a celebration feeling in the air. Our husbands cheer us on and tell us the winners crossed the finish line before all the runners got through the starting gate. Our little effort leaves me even more amazed by those that take part in full marathons.

*

Late in the previous school year, we had been approached by two of our local education authority advisors with a very unusual proposition. A young woman from another school had been very badly bullied by her headteacher and was on the verge of a breakdown. They felt she was a good teacher and they wanted to keep her in the profession but knew she would need her confidence restored.

I'd had some personal experience of the insidious way in which this kind of bullying can steal your self-confidence. A headteacher I'd worked for in the past, Ellen, was personable and had many strengths. We were a cohesive, hard-working and conscientious staff. Warm and friendly, her assemblies were often simple tales from her family life, easily accessible to the young children in our care. She encouraged teamwork and felt strongly that we should all have ownership of the new teaching practices that were being imposed from on high.

But you felt you knew, from comments made in the staff room, what she thought about everyone else apart from yourself. She wouldn't sign our planning, leading us to believe she never read it, or pass any comment on classroom displays or other aspects of our work, unless it was critical. She never observed my teaching but that didn't prevent her from having an opinion about it or making it clear that any problems I was having with difficult children were my fault.

She would ask for jobs to be done, which I would do immediately and with enthusiasm only to find she'd done them herself, tipping my efforts into the bin. There were lots of other petty little instances where my self-esteem could have been seriously undermined if it weren't for the refuge I had in God and the friends and family He's given me.

My current headteacher and I had a good reputation for mentoring students and NQT's (newly qualified teachers) so the advisors thought we might be ideal to help this young teacher. Pleased to have been asked and eager to help, we welcomed Rachel. She came to visit a couple of times before the summer and we began to form a relationship.   Now back in school for the new term, I discover that three more children have moved into our catchment area and we're now officially overcrowded. Because of Rachel, it's decided that I can take the extra children with her help.

After a day spent trying to plan, teach and manage 33 children and up to five adults in a relatively small classroom, in addition to my management responsibilities, I'm weary. It always seems to take a week or two to get my body back up to speed after the languor of a holiday. My phone rings.

'Mum, turn the news on. Terrorists have attacked America.' James' voice is breathless with shock.

I hurry home and watch, sickened and mesmerised, as the events unfold on TV. It's so much like a horror film, part of my brain hopes that if I watch long enough there will be some sort of conclusion and we'll learn that it hasn't been real.

I pray for the dead, the bereaved, the traumatised, world leaders and the world. I also lift before God the people so consumed by hatred and those that

fervently believe they're serving Him in this way. There is a sense that the
world is holding its breath, waiting to see what will happen next. The biased
and limited information given in the news is frustrating for a situation as
dangerous and complex as this one.

It feels perverse for ordinary life to carry on but, of course, it does. The
autumn term is always very busy in school. You forget how far you've come
with your previous class and it's a shock to grind yourself back, ready to start
over again.

We decide to split the class. Rachel takes the fifteen year-one children
into a tiny spare room and I keep the eighteen year-two children. She copes
extremely well and flourishes in the supportive atmosphere of our school.

The original arrangement had been for us to keep her for one term only
but I feel certain God's busy behind the scenes. The timing's perfect and
circumstances change as we go along until eventually Rachel becomes a
permanent and valued member of our staff.

*

'Can you both come over? We have something we need to tell you.'
Kenneth's voice is stiff and dark on the phone.

My stomach feels cold and twists painfully when we arrive at their
bungalow. Mum and Kenneth sit close together on the edge of their settee.
They look vulnerable and old. I don't want to hear what they have to say.

'We've seen the doctor today, for the results of the tests.' I can see the
World War II veteran in Kenneth's shoulders and straight back.

'You're mother has Alzheimer's.'

We're not surprised but sickened all the same.

Mum studies her hands writhing in her lap. She raises her face. It is full
of desperation.

'You must promise me you won't tell anyone.' Her eyes burn into us, as
she insists on our word. 'I don't want anyone to know,'

It won't be an easy promise to keep. Many already suspect things are not
right with Mum and they will only get worse. I'd found the support we'd

received from friends during James' illness, indispensable. Because we'd been open with our friends, they were able to share the burden with us. The awful stigma Mum imagines is connected to mental illness means she, and we, will be deprived of some of the support she might otherwise receive.

'Don't tell. Promise me.' Her words are fierce bullets. 'I don't want anyone to know.'

It's a promise I keep until she's past knowing, in the hopes that by sharing our experiences we can help reduce the stigma for others, that they and their carers might be less isolated.

*

At home, we push the spectre of Alzheimer's into a dark corner of our minds and get on. We try to decorate, build cupboards, alter things to suit our needs and generally make the new house 'ours'. At the last moment, we find a decorator who can give us three days only, before Christmas, which isn't quite enough.

After a hectic, work-related weekend in London with Howard, I finish the painting on Monday night, re-lay the carpet on Tuesday and move the furniture, books, etc back on Wednesday. Thursday night I'm out late at an office Christmas party and badminton on Friday, as I finish work for the holiday. On Saturday, in our 'wisdom', we've invited twenty-six people for a house-warming/Christmas dinner party. Just to make it more interesting, both of our boys arrive home for the holidays with all their many belongings and 'the great weatherman in the sky' dumps a load of snow and ice on us for good measure.

Strangely enough, no one wants to change the date for Christmas so we hit the floor running after the party to finish the shopping, wrapping, tidy up, prepare food, go to other parties and Howard still has to work on Monday. It's something of a surprise to find it's suddenly Christmas Day and after the big meal we collapse in a contented little heap.

Wishing to share our good fortune, we organise a surprise holiday for all of our family that live in the UK. Because our extended family is relatively large, for years we've come together over the New Year instead of Christmas itself. The Oasis holiday park is ideal for our party of twenty-one people, aged from three to seventy-six years old. Each family has its own accommodation and Howard has organised an itinerary of activities, which is optional and leaves each family with lots of time on their own as well as together. It's a blessing to be able to celebrate *en masse* and to see Mum blossom surrounded by her loving family.

In January, James confesses that he's having difficulty keeping track of the many hospital appointments he still has to attend. He asks me if I'll put them on my calendar then remind him of any that are pending when I phone for our regular Friday chat. This seems to work quite well until March, when there's some confusion over one of the dates. Suddenly, the penny drops.

'Oh, I remember now, that's the date of my heart operation.'

'What heart operation?' I manage to splutter into the phone. My own heart is doing belly flops into my churning stomach.

James reminds me of the Wolff-Parkinson-White syndrome they'd discovered during his diagnostic tests prior to chemotherapy. Now that James has been clear of cancer for five years, my adult son and his consultant have decided the time is right to correct the problem.

The operation involves threading various micro-cables into his heart from three different directions, locating the misfiring cluster and zapping them with a laser. Originally, they were going to do it as a day patient and I'm not sure James would even have told us; he's so very casual about it all. In the end the doctor decides that James is having too many palpitations for it to be safe so puts him on beta-blockers for a month in preparation for the surgery.

James may be casual about heart operations but I'm not. Bizarre nightmares fill my head the night before. I'm definitely not wanted at the hospital so James' girlfriend will ring me at work to let me know how he's gone on. When my headteacher, looking like she's seen a ghost, comes into my classroom an hour earlier than expected to say there's a phone call for me, I'm more than a little trepidatious. It's James.

'The good news is I'm still alive,' he chirpily informs me, 'the bad news is there's been an administrative error and I'll have to wait for up to a month.'

Because of his amputation and all the complications that made it difficult for him to use his prosthesis, James is able to have a car through the motobility scheme. During the wait for the operation, and in the middle of a week of crucial exams, his car is stolen. Someone put a brick through the frosted glass next to the front door, at half past three in the morning, picked up the keys and drove off before any of the lads were fully awake.

The next day, James' roommate set off to see the landlord about replacing all the door locks (the house keys being with the car keys), only to discover James' car parked a few streets away. They inform the police who put it under surveillance but give up after a while. The police ask to take the car in for forensic tests then charge James £138 to get it back. This outrageous fine on top of the cost of a new window, new steering lock, new locking system in the car, taxis to get to his police project in Wakefield and the garage to pick up his vehicle, make it very difficult for James to sleep for several weeks.

In spite of the trauma, he passes his exams and just misses a distinction by four marks. James also manages to enjoy the intense five-week project in social medicine, working alongside the police and finding out where most of his future patients will come from. The crime files are so horrific he can't bring himself to tell us anything about them and it's clear he's appalled to discover the deprivation and horrors some people endure here in our own country.

Eventually, James does have his operation. Howard and I go to visit him a few hours afterwards and find him in a bed tucked round the corner behind a glass partition separating him from the corridor. He is pale and sleepy.

'I had to be awake for the procedure so I asked if I could watch.' There is a slight sheen of sweat on his forehead that belies his bravado.

'It was more painful than I expected,' he confesses. He looks away.

I fuss him and we offer treats we've brought to cheer him up.

'I have to stay in bed for twenty-four hours because there are only blood clots holding the various entry points closed.'

I can see his imagination working overtime on that one, as he moves gingerly about on his bed. We don't stay long and he sleeps most of time before his discharge.

Meanwhile, David's really enjoying his course and developing skills he hopes will lead to a career in filmmaking. Howard's able to offer him a couple of opportunities to make corporate videos for his company and David does an excellent job on them.

It's fun to watch all the festivities around the Queen's Golden Jubilee. It brings back memories of our trip to London during the Silver Jubilee, when we'd tried unsuccessfully to convince the government to let me stay in the UK. Now, it feels like the great, vast, silent majority of this country is lumbering to its feet and showing the world that they can have a good time without any trouble, they're pleased to live here and proud of their hardworking, dedicated Queen. We have a Jubilee tea party at school with the children and it's marvellous to be part of it. Between that and the World Cup Football, I've never seen such patriotism in this country.

We have reason to celebrate in our family, too. Our 'baby', David, reaches twenty-one and graduates. We drop him off at the designated building on the morning of his graduation, and go to park the car. Lincoln is packed with parents and their young adult children. There's a buzz trembling off the cobbles of the old part of the city. Searching for David in a large, grand old building, I suddenly turn and there he is, grown-up and handsome in his cap and gown. Unexpectedly, tears spring to my eyes. Having missed my own graduation ceremony, I'm surprised to find how emotional I feel.

Perched on the edge of the hard pew, packed in with all the other proud, excited relatives, I peer into the gloom of Lincoln Cathedral. It's a magnificent building, awesome in its scale and history. And my little boy is called to the front to receive his diploma. In amongst the swirl of emotions, goose bumps tickle my arm and I realise I feel admiration. David has quietly and with no fuss got on and achieved his goal.

*

The dreadfully cruel illness that is Alzheimer's continues its relentless progress in Howard's mum. She doesn't become mean or aggressive, as some do, rather a few of her inhibitions are lost and she's more loving and demonstrative. Her main problem is increasing anxiety, as she tries so hard to cling to what she knows as 'herself'. She constantly asks questions, over and over, and demands answers, trying desperately to remember the basic building blocks of her life. It's like watching her slowly drowning and being unable to offer any comfort or reassurance.

To compound the challenge for Kenneth, macular degeneration is beginning to steal his vision. This is a disease of the eye which in his case rapidly progresses, leaving him registered blind in a relatively short period of time. He's always been a fit, active and independent man and this is a brutal blow. Now he's unable to drive, golf or carve the beautiful walking sticks that are his pride and joy. Mum wakes him as many as seven times a night, anxious and confused, unable to remember how to get back into bed. His life is reduced to sitting and holding her hand most afternoons in an attempt to calm her.

We try to help as much as we can. Howard sits with Mum so Kenneth can go out with friends a few evenings a month and I take her to church so he can have Sunday mornings off. Determined to keep her at home for as long as possible, Kenneth persists in the face of Mum's distress and she goes to respite care for one day a week but it's not enough. Their GP doesn't seem to be able to offer anything to help with the anxiety or broken nights.

Once again, Matthew and Alison's visit is a catalyst for action. We are all as worried about Kenneth, now, as Mum. We look into selling our house and buying something with a granny flat but Kenneth doesn't think it will work, as their needs increase and become more complex. I take Mum out for the day while Kenneth, Howard and his siblings investigate nursing homes. I have to lie to her every five minutes or so as she asks where Kenneth is and what he's doing.

Howard comes back with stories of smelly, dirty places, of care workers that seem at best indifferent, of patients like sacks of human refuse slumped in chairs. We don't really know what we're looking for. In the end we choose a clean, modern home recently built in the small town Mum has lived in all her life. We reason that it is close enough for Kenneth and her friends to visit easily.

I make her a simple photograph book with snaps of each member of ·her family and a potted history. She loves photos and I hope it will provide prompts for her memory and enable carers and visitors to have more meaningful conversations with her

Howard and I collect Mum and Kenneth and drive them to the home. Kenneth tries to explain to Mum what is happening a few minutes before we arrive. She doesn't understand what he's talking about.

The home is decorated in neutral tones and tactile fabrics. There are dramatic flower arrangements and it might have been a hotel except for the faint underlying odours of age and incontinence. We settle Mum into her room, placing items from home to make it more familiar. Then we take her down to the sitting room where there are other people to keep her company. We've been warned not to visit for a week or two to enable her to adjust. I am both afraid and longing to leave. I suspect Howard and Kenneth feel the same. Kenneth wraps his arms around her and says goodbye. At last, she understands.

'You can't leave me here,' she pleads. 'I've had six children. Is there no one to care for me?' Her cry shreds my heart and blisters my ears, as we hurry to the car. I know I shall hear it for the rest of my life when I think of Mum.

The home is a disaster. The staff are not trained to work with Alzheimer sufferers and are unable to meet Mum's special needs. They seem to try to fill her up with drugs and complain that she won't stay in bed at night. I arrive to visit one afternoon and squeeze past a crowd of employees in the foyer chatting over a delivery of boxes. As I press the code into the security pad, the door unlocks and I'm met by a little old woman scurrying down the corridor on her Zimmer frame.

'Someone's trapped! Someone's trapped!'

She's so upset that it takes a while to work out what the problem is. Eventually, I realise there is someone locked in the toilet and that someone is Mum. This is the last straw. We've struggled with Mum's clothes and shoes going missing, the lack of stimulating activities for the patients and their complaints about Mum but it's clear that this isn't the best place for her.

Eventually we find a more appropriate care home. It's an older building and two bus rides each way for Kenneth but it's wonderful. I am in awe of the people who work there. They treat their confused, disabled patients, and their grieving family members, with so much love, respect and care that, unbelievably, it's a joy to visit and spend time amongst them. Mum's obvious contentment and cared for appearance eases the terrible guilt Howard and I feel and reassures us that we've made the right choice for them both.

*

May 2004

'Do you still want to leave teaching?'

My heart brakes sharply then bunny hops like a learner driver back into rhythm. I've always loved teaching but am gradually finding it harder and harder to summon the energy to keep abreast of the incessant changes, the patience for the children or the passion I once knew. Wary that these new feelings weren't from God but just an unhealthy temptation brought on by Howard's remarkable success, I've been fighting hard to get my fervour back. Despite all the praise and support given and the clear signs that I'm doing a good and effective job, I still feel increasingly unhappy.

Various opportunities have presented themselves. Headship's an obvious next step, the English advisor has encouraged me to apply for an advisor's post and the teacher training college has offered me a job release to lecture to student teachers. I'm flattered and uplifted by these offers but none of them feel right. For the last few years, I've prayed for guidance, discussed and debated the issues with Howard and other close friends.

I'm not sure what else I could do. An avid reader, I would love to be an author. But writing has always seemed like something only special, rare and gifted people could hope to do, something wholly unattainable for me. I don't know any authors. I enjoy writing but don't feel particularly creative. I've had a letter read out on Terry Wogan's radio programme and an article published in the Gideon's magazine, not much to base a new career on. A tutor, working with me on a Master's module in education, declared that 'at least you can write'. I've tried a correspondence course but found I just couldn't give it the time and attention it needed. Perhaps, with no pressure to earn a living or raise children...

'Do you really mean it?' I'm at the peak of a roller coaster gripping hold of the brake, do I dare? I search Howard's face. I can see he's in the seat right next to me and I love him for believing in me.

'I'll ring my union to see what I have to do.'

I'm told my letter of resignation has to be handed in by tomorrow, if I want to go at the end of the school year in two months time. I sit down and start typing.

Tears sting at the back of my eyes, when I hand my letter to Judith. I think of all the difficulties we've faced together, all that we've achieved. We're friends as well as trusted colleagues. She has always been so kind and supportive. I know she'll find it as hard to let me go as I'm finding it to leave.

Judith wraps me in her arms. She knows me well enough not to be truly surprised.

'It'll be all right.' There are tears in her smile.

The next day Howard, David and I set off on a walking holiday in northern Spain. We've never been on this type of organised trip before and it's fantastic. There are seventeen people, from all over the world and different walks of life, and we all mould together easily. The only decision I have to make is what to have in my sandwich. Every day's walking is different, full of splendour and interest. The accommodation, food and company are all superb. The tensions of the previous months begin to melt away. I feel wonderful.

As we walk and talk, friendships are formed. One couple, who are consultants for eco-tourism and write travel books, help me to believe that becoming a writer could be achievable, a musician, involved in publishing

Christian music, tells me to let him know when I've written something and he'll see if he can help me get published.

Back home, the old insecurities swamp me. What have I done? Driving to church in the morning, I'm suddenly flooded with the certainty that this *is* what God wants me to do. I can almost feel Him laughing at me as the light dawns. Does He always have to hit me with a sledgehammer before I realise he's answering my prayers? He's providing the opportunities and the encouragement to go for the unattainable, He's almost assured me of guaranteed success, all I have to do is get writing and trust in Him.

The service at church is about the Holy Spirit. I'm restless with frustration. It's all theory and no real life examples. As I sit thinking about all the experiences I've had of the Spirit in my life and how the personal stories of others have always been so uplifting to me, I begin to become excited. This title arrives fully formed in my head. I've never started with a title before.

As more people become aware of my plans to leave teaching and try my hand at writing, the encouragement floods in. The theme at the house group meeting is exactly related to what I'm experiencing and I feel prompted to share what's happening in my life, requesting prayer support. More and more the responses are that I should write my story. On the first day of the summer holidays, I sit down and the words begin to come.

*

April 2005

I try to hide my crinkled nose in a smile of greeting. The carer turns to lock the door behind me, a solid barrier against the fresh spring breeze outside. Over-warm air, heavy with smoke, industrial strength cleaning products and the indignity of adults in nappies, encases me.

Signing the fire regulation, black-bound and lined visitor's book recalls a memory. From ages past, I see a simpler book on whose pristine pages my mother had painted evocative, miniature watercolours to cheer her friends. Her life had finished before all the pages received their joyful reminiscences. A tragedy and yet...

Through another locked door I greet a wraith, mumbling and loitering near this escape route. He brings his face within an inch of mine. Puffing and blowing, his breath is sour and his manner threatening to the uninformed. I shake his hand reassuringly and say his name. The skin feels cool even in this warm place and stretched smooth across the bony fingers. He smiles and turns away.

Peeping into a small lounge, the curtains clean but pulled awry, my eyes rest on a wheelchair bound soul with sightless eyes in a saggy, basset hound face. His hands are cupped together on his lap. 'Sweetie please?' he says.

'Sorry, Fred, I don't have any sweeties today,' I reply sadly.

The other occupant, a long lean man dressed in a rugby shirt, his distorted frame supported by brightly coloured cushions and a child's cow shaped furry backpack. In his silent world, chin locked onto his chest, even smiles are denied. His wife, so often by his side, is not there today and concern for her recurring bouts of depression flares across my mind.

I am drawn then to the far end of the long corridor, past the staff room. Recollections of a hundred tiny kindnesses, a gentle kiss, a cuddle, a dignity respected, lift my spirits.

Determined, Rose plods past me on her never ending circuit of the passageway. Her hand grips the safety rail that runs its length. I shout a greeting and smile.

'Eh? What'd you say?' she bellows in return.

'Hello Rose,' I raise my voice another decibel and smile as widely as I can.

In the large L-shaped lounge I notice the new carpet and an elderly man trying to pick the pattern off. The ragged armchairs have been replaced with stylish, matching ones and I feel grateful that these things are deemed important but not at the expense of the care given.

Wartime music is pulsing loudly and Hattie swishes up to me with an infectious but toothless grin. I bend, as she presses her soft, road-map-lined forehead to mine and says, 'Do you want to dance, Sally?'

Holding her hand, I sway and smile encouragingly. She lifts her skirt above her knees and dances a little dance for me, all the time telling tall tales about Charlie and Sally and whispering about the mischief we used to get up to. Then she moves away to another Sally or Charlie, lighting dark corners with her bright memories.

At last I spot the one I seek. She's in a corner asking incomprehensible questions to one unable to answer. Her fingers work incessantly, brow furrowed deeply and scarred where she's fallen in her anxiety, rushing nowhere on frail legs.

'Hello Mum,' I say gently, touching her arm and bending to place my face in her narrow line of vision.

'Ahhh,' she smiles, as she sees that I am one of hers.

'Shall we go up to your room?' I ask, leading her towards the locked door. One of the cheerful carers struggles with a cluster of keys to let us out.

'How's life clipping you?' she asks.

'I'm fine Mum,' making sure I smile because the words have no meaning now.

'One of the, I was going to say, what are?' she asks, her body language indicating she wants an answer.

'This lift is noisy,' I reply. Her muscles are tense and the fingers are still chattering away.

'Thought you were making yourself dilling.'

'Come on Mum, let's go into the lift.' There is no recognition of her image in the large mirror that dominates the tiny space.

She cannot understand my directions and resists physical prompts so it takes ages to negotiate our way to her room. It is clean and tidy, photographs of her children and grandchildren dotted around. Her mattress is on the floor so that when she falls out in the night she won't hurt herself. Bars would only frighten her. A soft throw over the two-seat settee, a pretty cushion and teddy bears are tactile attempts to comfort and reach into her muddled mind.

'I've looked at that miline one,' she tells me.

'Shall we sit here for a while, Mum,' I suggest, sitting down and trying to gently manoeuvre her beside me.

'We'll have to be adrose together.' For a moment she is quiet and looks at the floor, as if lost.

'It's a lovely day, Mum.'

'Oh hello, luv. I keep forgetting.' She smiles, seeing me, as if for the first time. 'How are for?'

I tell her in snatches about her son and other family news using pictures to help her remember but it has gone. She can only listen in tiny bursts but chatters happily, her muscles slowly relaxing, her hands finally still.

The photos and her hands remind me of the long hours of work she did in the mills and at home rearing six children. The muscular calves made large from walking miles in the Yorkshire hills and valleys have disappeared from her skeletal frame. The gaunt face barely resembles her smiling one captured in the photographs.

Her heart was more than equal to making room for me, the other wives and husbands and the many grandchildren. I remember her saying that it was important for parents to have a regular time together, backed up by the offer of free babysitting. I can hear her laughter and smell the roast chicken, mashed potatoes and gravy, puddings swimming in custard that we often shared on those Friday nights before we went out. Her common sense advice, only ever offered on request, support and encouragement filled the void of my own mother's loss.

'Can I have some artimicial?' she asks.

I search in her drawer and find some chocolate.

'Mmmm,' she murmurs as I put a piece into her mouth. She gives me a chocolaty, coquettish grin.

'Is that nice?' I giggle with her.

'They seem very enjoyed by each other,' she adds.

As she tires, I take her back downstairs where she will be whisked into her pyjamas by skilled hands.

Mum smiles into the familiar face of the friendly carer and forgets that I've been.

I know better than to say goodbye, as the ache of parting would remain even if she couldn't remember why. I wait beside the locked door to be set free, sign myself out and hurry back into the springtime.

*

Summer 2005

James is home. But there's something wrong. He's like a toy with dead batteries. Due to set off on a long holiday, I'm frantic. Backed into a corner, he finally tells me that he and his girlfriend have split up.

'But, why? What happened?' My head is spinning. The happily-ever-after scenario I'd imagined for James and the perfect Maggie lies smashed at my feet. I look at him. He's broken. He can't talk about it.

I board the plane, with Howard and a chest full of guilt and worry, certain I'm abandoning my child when he needs me most. My sleep over the next few weeks is peppered with nightmares. I'm a little shocked by my reaction. This has never happened before, when girls have come and gone from my sons' lives.

James met Maggie three years earlier. He'd been persuaded to take an extra year of study to work with a research team investigating a treatment for bladder cancer. Maggie was on an exchange course at his university. She was Polish by birth but grew up in Germany. Fluent in five languages, she was studying genetic molecular biology. Slim and blonde, she was also gentle, polite and loving. She fitted effortlessly into the family. James seemed more relaxed, more complete, when they were together. For Christmas, he wrote and illustrated a children's story for her and had it translated into Polish, the language of her childhood.

They'd been separated the following year. James was caught up in his medical studies and Maggie had to return to her university in Freiburg. They found it very difficult to be apart. James started taking German night classes and arranged to do another extra year studying medicine in Germany.

Howard and I visited them in October and met Maggie's parents. James and Maggie translated between us all and I was amazed at my son's mastery of a new language in such a short time. Despite the communication barrier, we parents all got on very well. At one point we learned that Maggie's dad laughs in his sleep, which nicely sums up the nature of the man. Her mother had brought a beautiful and elaborate cake for James' birthday and fussed over him, as if he were her own.

Ask any parent what they want for their child and the answer will probably be some version of 'happiness'. This relationship promised comfortable love, rewarding and challenging careers and few, if any, in-law problems. If arranged marriage was part of our culture, I would have chosen this young woman for my son. I thought he was safely sorted.

Back home it becomes clear to me that this is much more than a broken relationship. My normally hyperactive, gregarious son is listless, he can barely get out of bed and he's avoiding his friends. James' life has suffered a stress fracture.

We talk and argue. I can't let it go. I read books and trawl the internet for information on depression, anxiety and obsessive compulsive disorder. Gradually, my brave son begins to rebuild himself. He goes to doctors and tries out a behaviour therapy programme he found on the internet. Through sheer strength of character, he picks up his final year of medical studies and becomes a doctor. I piece together what I think has happened.

From personal experience, I know how hard it can be to live in a different country from the one you've grown up in. Even between countries with the same language there are cultural differences. I often feel just outside the circle of everyone else. I don't share common childhood experiences with my peers, struggled for decades to understand British humour and still approach social cheek kisses stiffly. My first year, when Howard was the only person I was close to in the whole country, had been enormously challenging. And I am more at ease with my own company than James, who has always needed friends around.

In Germany, James was trying to study a difficult subject in a language he was still learning. Cut off from his own friends and family, he was entirely reliant on his relationship with Maggie. The cracks created by this pressure, I believe, released suppressed post traumatic stress symptoms buried at the time of his cancer and amputation.

Looking back, I think people, myself included, made things harder for James by insisting that he was brave and inspirational. This must have made it impossible for him to admit or share the understandable fears and feelings he really felt, encouraging him to believe secretly that he was just a cowardly fraud. The truth is, the decisions he made and the things he did in the face of those fears were what made him brave and inspirational to the rest of us.

Months later, James confesses to having considered suicide. This is more frightening because there'd been no cry for help at the time. If he'd followed through with that impulse, he would have succeeded. I thank God he sought and found the assistance he needed to recover.

Postscript – August 2008

Be ready at all times to answer anyone who asks you to explain the hope you have in you, but do it with gentleness and respect. 1 Peter 3:15-16

Someone once explained to me that memoir is a story *from* a life and autobiography the story *of* a life. It's taken four years of draft after draft to write this memoir of James' illness and the profound impact it had on our lives. But this is more than that. I long to show the relevance of faith, the difference it can make in crisis, in the everyday and in times of great joy.

And it's been twelve years since we faced James' diagnosis of cancer. He's home again briefly, doing locum work before he starts his next contract. His girlfriend, Wanyi, a doctor like James, has been refused an extension to her visa after seven years in this country and is going back home to Singapore. James is going with her. Selfishly, I hope it won't be a permanent move.

David and Anna, his Finnish girlfriend, have settled in Lincoln. He's making the films he loves and is very happy. I ask him what it is with my boys and their foreign girls.

'We're just following in Dad's footsteps,' he replies, with a wicked grin.

Mum passed away after two years in the nursing home. We filled the church with photos and memories and celebrated her life. Kenneth, now registered blind and in his eighties, recently faced surgery for cancer. The doctors wouldn't normally do this operation on a man of his age but when he told them he'd done a seven-mile walk with us over New Year, they took a chance. He's bounced back quickly, taken up bowling again, is still making new friends and greeting each day with a smile.

Howard's company was sold a year ago and he's learning to embrace retirement. It's tempting to join him but there are stories in me bursting to be told. I've had so much to learn about the craft of writing and I've loved every minute of it. Even in the rejections, I've heard whispers of how to improve.

When my writing teacher returned my first draft with positive comments and areas to work on, I was emptied. In my brain, I knew there would be much more work to do but it felt like I'd reached the summit of a great mountain only to find hundreds more behind that I still had to climb.

I almost gave up. From nowhere a woman I hadn't spoken to in years, phoned and invited me to speak to a church group about my work. It was all I needed to get started again. And every time I've faltered since then, God has sent something – a small success, the right word, an invitation to speak – to keep me going. I look forward to seeing what He has in store for me next.